UNIT 1

1 Airport words

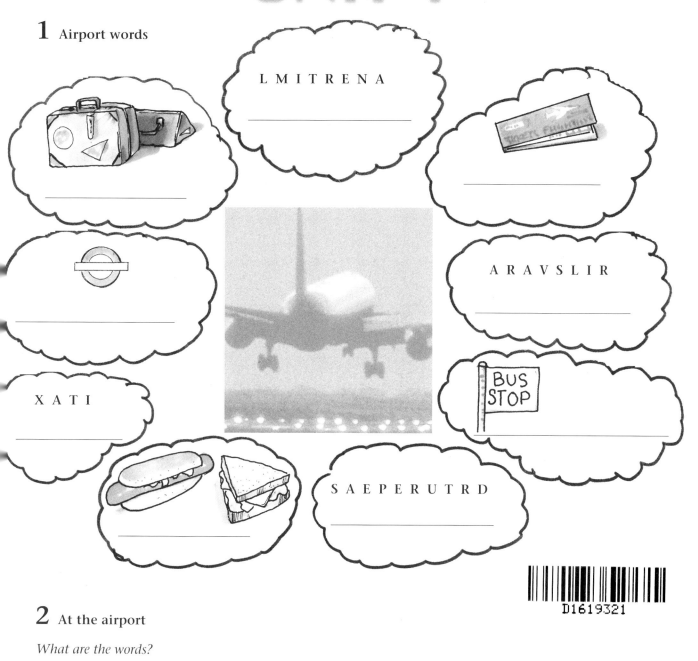

L M I T R E N A

A R A V S L I R

X A T I

S A E P E R U T R D

2 At the airport

What are the words?

1

3 Instruments

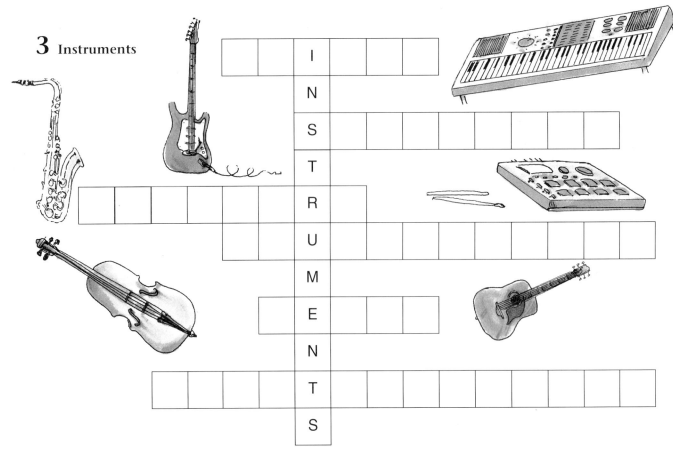

4 What can you hear?

Write[1] the words down.

1. a girl
2.
3.
4.
5.
6.
7.
8.
9.
10.

[1][raɪt] *schreiben*

5 a or an?

..rp.rt — an airport

sn.ck b.r

.nstr.m.nt

.nt.rv..w

h.t.l

d..r

s.x.ph.n.

| CHECK-IN | STEP A | STEP B | STEP C | TRACK | CHECK-OUT |

1 Hello!   Write in the answers.

1. Hello, what's your name?
   _____   My name's Max.

2. Hello, where are you from?
   _____   Yes, I am.

3. Hello, Tarkan. Are you English?
   _____   I'm from Islington.

4. Hello, Maike. Are you from Neunkirchen?
   _____   No, I'm not.

5. Hello, Mrs Harrison-Haber. Are you Tarkan's mother[1]?
   _____   No, I'm not.

[1]['mʌðə] *Mutter*

2 Welcome to Islington

Put in[1]:   your   it is   I'm   it isn't   you're   is

1. Hello, _____ Tony Clifton. _____ from Islington.

2. Hi, _____ Tarkan. – _____ Tarkan a German name? – No, _____ . It's Turkish.

3. Is it _____ saxophone? – Yes, _____ . Wow, _____ lucky[2]!

[1][ˌpʊt ˈɪn] *(ein)setzen*   [2]['lʌki] *glücklich (sein)*

3 From word to word

3 – 5 words: OK!
6 – 8 words: Great[1]!

pilottttt taxiiiiii instrumentsssss ?

[1][ɡreɪt] *super, spitze*

4 Words with o

Look[1] *at page*[2] *9 in your English book*[3]. *Put the words with an o in the right list.*

[əʊ]	[ə]	[ʊ]
go	Islington	_____
_____	_____	_____
_____	_____	[ɒ]
_____	_____	_____

[1][lʊk] *schauen, sehen*   [2][peɪdʒ] *Seite*   [3][bʊk] *Buch*

5 I – you – he – she – it – we – they?

1. Look, that's Maike. _____'s from Germany.
2. That's Tony Clifton. _____'s from Islington.
3. Hello, _____'m Tarkan.
4. Here are Maike and Sebastian. _____'re singers.
5. Hi, Max! Are _____ the boy with the two instruments?
6. OK, boys and girls. Let's go. _____'re in England now.
7. What about the keyboard? No, _____'s a drum computer.

6 One and lots of

one	lots of
name	
	T-shirts
band	
	friends
singer	
	guitars
window	
	interviews

7 Word bank[1]

Look at the word list in your English book.

people[2]	places[3]	transport[4]	music
1. boy	airport	taxi	saxophone
2.			
3.			
4.			
5.			
6.			
7.			
8.			

[1][bæŋk] [2]['pi:pl] *Menschen, Leute* [3]['pleɪs(ɪz)] *Ort(e)* [4]['trænspɔ:t]

8 Numbers

You say	You write	The number is	You say	You write	The number is
[faɪv]	five	5	[ˌfɪf'ti:n]		
['sevn]			[ˌθɜː'ti:n]		
[eɪt]			['twenti]		
[θriː]			[ˌfɔː'ti:n]		
[naɪn]			[ˌtwenti 'sɪks]		

9 [s] or [z] ?

Write the words in the 's' or 'z' box¹.

pilots   girls   tickets   cars
doors   car parks   friends
instruments   names   airports

pilots _____
_____
_____
_____

girls _____
_____
_____
_____

¹[bɒks] *Kasten*

10 What are the words?

Write them down in your exercise¹ book. Example: thirteen, …

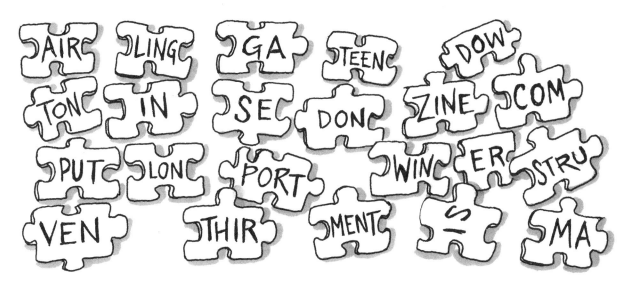

¹['eksəsaɪz] *Übung(s-)*

11 One word and two words

Look at the word list in your English book.

1. picture and *picture dictionary* _____
2. car and _____
3. drum and _____
4. saxophone and _____
5. city and _____
6. snack and _____
7. bus and _____
8. check and _____
9. coffee and _____
10. hotel and _____
11. school and _____

1 The band

Write down the right sentences in your exercise book.

1. Maike 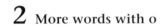 a Turkish name.
2. Max's two instruments — the electric guitar.
3. Sebastian — is — a singer too.
4. Sandra's two instruments — the guitar and the keyboard.
5. Sebastian's instrument — are — the bandleader and a singer.
6. Tarkan — 'The Good Vibes'.
7. The name of the band — the saxophone and the cello.
8. Tarkan's instrument — the drum computer.

2 More words with o

Say these words. Then put them in the right lists.

too	Tony	one	school	window	lot	reporter
you	shop	door	computer	lot	hello	from
go	keyboard	stronger	four	stop	hot dog	cello
airport	pilot	mother	not	more	two	hotel

[ɒ]	[ɔː]	[əʊ]	[ə]	[uː]
shop	*four*	*go*	*pilot*	*two*
				[ʌ]

3 The right order[1]

Write the sentences in your exercise book.

1. the / is / cello. / on / Max
2. not / German / is / a / Tarkan / name.
3. from / They / all / one / school. / are
4. instruments. / names / The / on / not / are / the
5. of / the / the / What's / band? / name
6. smile. / a / give / German / The / friends / Nicola / little

[1] [ˈɔːdə] *Reihenfolge*

4 More words

Write two or more words.

1. cello, guitar, _____
2. car, taxi, _____
3. Tessa, _____
4. snack, _____
5. London, _____
6. arrivals, _____
7. _____

5 I / my – you / your

1. Hello, _____ name is Tony Clifton and _____'m from Islington.
2. Hello, bandleader. What's _____ name?
3. Where are _____ from, Tarkan? Are _____ from Germany?
4. Hello, welcome to _____ minibus!
5. _____'m a singer and _____ instrument is the electric guitar.

6 The friends from Germany

Make sentences. Write them in your exercise book.

Hello, my _____
That's _____ name.
My instrument _____

7 Write it down in English

1. Hallo, bist du das Mädchen aus Islington?
2. Islington ist in London.
3. Tony Clifton ist aus Islington.
4. Ist Nicola eine Reporterin?
5. Maike und Sandra sind die zwei Mädchen in der Band.
6. Maike ist eine Sängerin.
7. Tarkan ist kein deutscher Name.
8. Unsere Namen sind auf unseren T-Shirts.
9. Ist Sebastian auch ein Sänger?
10. Der Name der Band ist *The Good Vibes*.
11. Wir sind alle in der gleichen Schule.

1

1 Silent letters

Listen to the words (again and again). Find the silent[1] letter or letters. (You can't hear[2] them!)

Example: nam~~e~~

five	please	magazine	saxophone	welcome
nine	eleven	seven	two	guitar
		eight	right	

[1] ['saɪlənt] *stumm* [2] [hɪə] *hören*

2 Numbers

Write the next[1] three numbers. Be careful! There is a system[2].

1. eleven, twenty-two, thirty-three, _____

2. sixty-three, seventy, seventy-three, _____

3. fifty-two, fifty-six, sixty, _____

4. ninety-six, ninety, eighty-four, _____

5. fourteen, twenty-eight, forty-two, _____

6. ninety-eight, eighty-seven, seventy-six, _____

7. three, twenty-five, forty-seven, _____

[1] [nekst] *nächste(r/s)* [2] ['sɪstəm]

3 More numbers

Write down these numbers in words.

4	_____	5	_____	8	_____
14	_____	15	_____	18	_____
40	_____	50	_____	80	_____
44	_____	55	_____	88	_____

4 A word game   *Can you go on?*

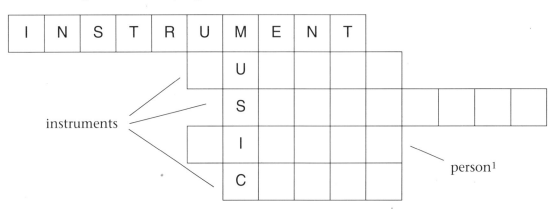

[1] ['pɜːsn]

8 *eight*

1 The ...ty family[1]

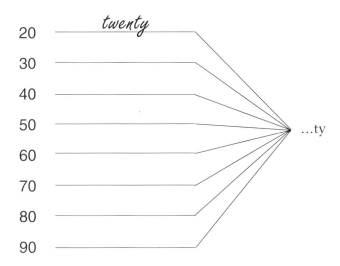

20 — twenty
30 —
40 —
50 — ...ty
60 —
70 —
80 —
90 —

[1]['fæmli] *Familie* [2][ˌplʌgˈɪn] *(ein)stecken*

"Hey, where can I plug in[2] my keyboard?"

2 The people in the band

Here are the answers. But what are the questions?

1. Yes, we are all from one school. _____
2. My instrument is the drum computer. _____
3. Yes, I'm a singer too. _____
4. No, it's a Turkish name. _____
5. Yes, she's our teacher. _____
6. We're 'The Good Vibes'. _____

3 Is or are?

1. A girl _____ the bandleader.
2. Max _____ the boy with two instruments.
3. Sandra and Maike _____ the two girls in the band.
4. The boy on the right _____ Tarkan.
5. _____ Maike and Sebastian singers?
6. Tony Clifton _____ in his bus.
7. The German friends _____ in the bus too.
8. The instruments _____ OK.
9. Tony _____ careful with the instruments.
10. _____ the windows open?

4 The first[1] two words

1. _____ _____ the bandleader, Maike?
2. _____'s _____ name of your band?
3. _____ _____ your instruments, Max?
4. _____ _____ good time here in Islington.
5. _____ _____ a Turkish name?
6. _____ _____ for the interview!

[1][fɜːst] *erste(r/s)*

| CHECK-IN | STEP A | STEP B | STEP C | TRACK | **CHECK-OUT** |

1

1 Words and numbers

Write the words down in the singular form, then write the number (2 – 9) and the plural form.

1. weiertvni   _interview_   (2) _two interviews_
2. itktce   _____   (3) _____
3. iaxt   _____   (4) _____
4. rniestmnut   _____   (5) _____
5. ragtiu   _____   (6) _____
6. iwdnwo   _____   (7) _____
7. eirdnf   _____   (8) _____
8. ructipe   _____   (9) _____

2 More pronouns

1. Hello. _____'m Tony. _____'m from Islington.
2. That's Maike. _____'s the bandleader.
3. Are _____ in Islington now?
4. Hello, Sandra. Are _____ the keyboarder?
5. That's Max. _____'s on the cello.
6. And that's Nicola. _____'s a reporter for a magazine.

3 The people in Unit 1

Write down the three missing¹ words.

1. _____ _____ _____ are from Islington.
2. The guitar and the _____ _____ _____ instruments.
3. Tarkan _____ _____ _____ name.
4. Maike is the bandleader and _____ _____ _____ .
5. Sebastian and Maike _____ _____ _____ singers.
6. Nicola _____ _____ _____ for the school magazine.

¹['mɪsɪŋ] *fehlende(r/s)*

4 A Unit 1 alphabet

A arrival, _____   J just   S save, _____
B boy, _____   K keyboard, _____ T ticket, _____
C cello, _____   l lots, _____   U Underground
D door, _____   M minibus, _____   V vibes
E electric, _____   N new, _____   W window, _____
F friend, _____   O on, _____   X – – –
G go, _____   P photo, _____   Y you, _____
H hello, _____   Q question   Z – – –
I it, _____   R right, _____

10 *ten*

UNIT 2

1 What's this?

Look at the pictures and write down what the things are.

It is a _____

They are _____

2 What can you see there?

Write: There is … /
There are …

1. What can you see in the window?

2. … on the roof?

3. … in the garden?

4. … in the minibus?

5. … under the tree?

| CHECK-IN | **STEP A** | STEP B | STEP C | TRACK | CHECK-OUT |

1 Look and see

This is Tarkan's room at the Cliftons' house. Write about the things in his room and say where the things are when you can.

Start: There is ... / There are ...
Or: There is / are no ... in his room.

[1][tɔɪz] *Spielzeuge*

| bed | cupboard | table | chair | window | picture | flowers | magazine |
| box | toys[1] | map | in | on | under | wall | |

2 Tessa's things

[1]diary ['daɪəri] *Tagebuch*

a) *How many of these things has Tessa got in her room?*

She's got one _____

one _____

two _____

_____

_____

_____

and _____

b) *Has she got a hobby?* _____

3 At home with the Cliftons

[1][əˈlɜːdʒɪk] [2][beə]

Put in 'has got' / 'have got' or 'hasn't got' / 'haven't got'.

The Cliftons _____ a big house. They _____ a big garage too, for the car and the minibus. The minibus is Mrs Clifton's. She _____ a shop with Mr Braden in Islington High Street. Mr Clifton _____ a job in the City. The Cliftons _____ three children now, so Mr and Mrs Clifton _____ a lot of time. They _____ a new baby. His name is Tim. It's nice for Tim – he _____ a big sister (Tessa, 13) and a big brother (Jake, 7), and they can play with him after school. And Jake _____ a lot of old toys for his little brother. Tarkan _____ the baby's room now. (The baby is very small and he _____ a small bed in Mr and Mrs Clifton's bedroom.) They _____ a dog or a cat because Jake is allergic[1] – but Jake _____ a very big teddy bear[2].

4 Jake's jokes[1]

Jake is a silly boy.

a) *Put in the right words.*

① I can put these things where _____ the others can't find them.

② Mum! Where's _____ teddy bear. I can't find it.

③ And where's _____ funny picture of _____ German teacher? She can't see it, it's too funny. Oh dear, where is it?
What's that, Tarkan? You can't find _____ map of London? Hm, that's funny: _____ mother can't find _____ maps. And Mum and Dad can't find _____ small TV[2]. It isn't in _____ bedroom.
Uh-oh! Jake again! But he can't find _____ teddy bear ...? Hah! That's _____ trick!

④ JAAAAKE!!!

⑤ It's OK, Tessa, the things are all in _____ bedroom! _____ the wall. _____ the cupboard. _____ the box of toys.

| my (4x) | your | his (2x) |
| her | our | their (2x) |

b) *Now look at the picture and finish Tarkan's sentences.*

[1][dʒəʊk] Spaß, Unfug [2][ˈtiːviː] Fernseher

5 My dream house

[dri:m] *Traum(-)*

a) *Make this a picture of your dream¹ house. Put in nice colours.*

b) *Now write down in your exercise book what your house has got and what colours the things are.*

Example: My house has got a red roof and a blue door. It has got a big garden with lots of …
Or: My dream house is very big. The walls are yellow. There's …

6 The Mannings and the Smiths

The Mannings have got a dog – look, here he is. And here.
Oh, no! You can't see him in this photo, he's in his house.
Kevin has got a mountain bike, look at it …

Sebastian is with the Manning family, and Max is with the Smiths. They have got photos of the families, and of their flat or house.

Write what is in the photos. Be careful! Is it 's or s'?

The Smiths have got a very big TV in their living room. And the girls are Boyzone fans – just look at their room!
This is a bad photo of Tracy, but you can see her in-line skates!

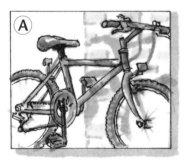

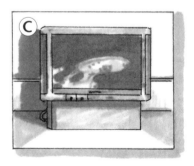

1 One or more

Write the plural forms.   child _____   way _____   woman _____

man _____   baby _____   box _____   boy _____

2 What's that funny sound? – Part III

Put the words (and sounds) in the right pictures.   ¹[kætʃ] *fangen* ²[ə'weɪ] *weg* ³[rʌn] *rennen*

"Hmm – what's that funny sound?"   "Miaow!"   "Miaow!"   "Hssssss!"

"Grrrrrr!"   "Bow-wow! Wuff!"   "Wuff! Wuff!"   "Ouwww!"

"Silly cat! I can catch¹ you."   "Max, this is ... Oh dear!"

"Come here, Milly, this is your new friend, Max."   "This is terrible! Now where can I go?"

"This is my place – go away²!"   "OK, Liam ..."   "Nice dog? Huh!"

"I know where you can't catch me."   "Ha! Now I'm OK – that silly dog can't do this."

"Please, Max, come down! Milly's a nice dog – you can be friends."

"Hey, Max! Come here – I'm your friend. You can't run³ away from a silly dog."

| CHECK-IN | STEP A | STEP B | **STEP C** | TRACK | CHECK-OUT |

1 What can you do?

[swɒp] (aus)tauschen

Write six questions with 'Can ...?'. *Example:*
Then swap¹ books with a Can your mother sing? – Yes, she can.
partner and write answers. Can you play the guitar? – No, but I can play the piano.

2 What's that (funny) sound? – Part IV

What words and names have got these sounds?
Be careful – three words / names can go in two
of the sound boxes.

	that	magazine	Wilson	with
they	mother	Elizabeth	sound	things
	the	bathroom	please	place
	house	Islington	three	thanks

[s]	[z]	[θ]	[ð]

3 Take care¹ of your street²

Stell dir vor, du hast ein Haus in Islington und es gibt Probleme in deiner Straße. Trage die Informationen in das Formular ein. Eine Islingtoner Adresse findest du auf Seite 17.

Example: There is a (big) hole³ in …
The … is broken⁴ / dirty⁵.

CARING FOR YOUR STREET

HELP US TO HELP YOU – Use this card⁶ to let us know⁷ about any problems in your street.

WHERE IS THE PROBLEM? Put in street name & number of nearest⁸ house.

Please tick⁹ problem		Please give more information or write about any other street problems here:
Street cleaning¹⁰ Dog mess¹¹ Graffiti Pavement¹² parking	Damaged¹³ pavement Street tree problems Street lights Street signs¹⁴	

Your name .... Tel. ....
Address ....

¹[teɪk ˈkeə] *Sorge tragen (für), sich sorgen (um)* ²[striːt] *Straße* ³[həʊl] *Loch*
⁴[ˈbrəʊkn] *zerbrochen* ⁵[ˈdɜːti] *schmutzig* ⁶[kɑːd] ⁷[nəʊ] *wissen* ⁸[ˈnɪərɪst] *nächstgelegene(r/s)* ⁹[tɪk] *abhaken, ankreuzen* ¹⁰[ˈkliːnɪŋ] *Reinigung* ¹¹[mes] *Dreck, Kot*
¹²[ˈpeɪvmənt] *Bürgersteig* ¹³[ˈdæmɪdʒd] *beschädigt* ¹⁴[saɪn] *(Straßen-)Schild*

4 The Islington game

You can play this game in small groups. Ihr braucht Würfel und Spielsteine. Es geht nicht darum, schnell fertig zu werden, sondern möglichst viele Punkte (*points*) zu sammeln.

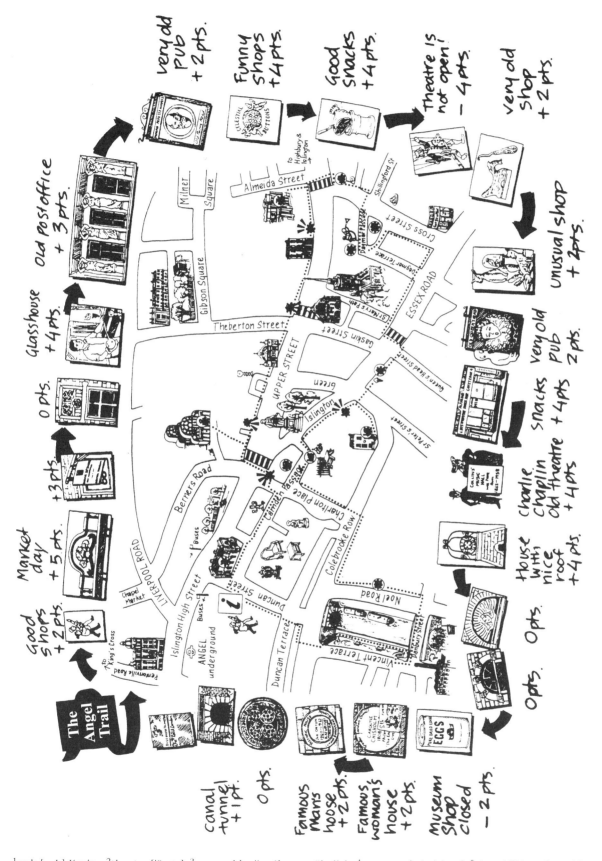

[1]pub [pʌb] *Kneipe* [2]theatre [ˈθɪətə] [3]unusual [ʌnˈjuːʒl] *ungewöhnlich* [4]museum [mjuːˈziːəm] [5]closed [ˈkləʊzd] *geschlossen* [6]famous [ˈfeɪməs] *berühmt* [7]canal tunnel [kəˈnæl ˈtʌnl] [8]market [ˈmɑːkɪt] [9]glasshouse [ˈɡlɑːshaʊs] [10]post office [ˈpəʊstˌɒfɪs] *Postamt*

1 What can you see in the picture

Start: I can see ... *Or:* There's ... / There are ... *Write the sentences down in your exercise book.*

2 Mr Braden's hobby

1. We are on a ... – the others are in the sky.
2. There are a lot of ... in the sky.
3. The ... of London are a problem for Mr Braden.
4. They are too ...
5. Mr Braden has got a very good ...
6. It's interesting to look at this with his (5).
7. Have you got a ... like Mr Braden?
8. ... he can't do his hobby – he hasn't got time, or it's too (4), or Sandra is in his room.
9. Where you can see (1), (2), and (6).
10. A very interesting hobby.

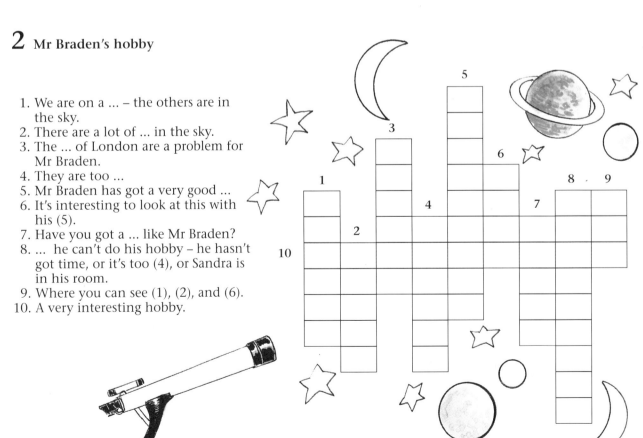

| CHECK-IN | STEP A | STEP B | STEP C | TRACK | CHECK-OUT |

1 Short answers

That's OK.	Why not?	Yes, there is.	No, there isn't.	OK!
That's nice.	What?	No problem.	I don't know.	Yes, you can.
No, you can't.	Sure.	Oh dear!	Good idea!	Yes, it is.
No, it isn't.	Thank you.	Oh, sorry!	Of course!	That's funny.
		Oh!	Thanks.	

What can you say? Es gibt mehrere Möglichkeiten. Kannst du jeweils zwei passende Antworten finden?

1. Can I look at your pictures, please? – _____ / _____
2. Hey, that's my bag! – _____ / _____
3. We're a German reggae band. – _____ / _____
4. Can we all go in the minibus? – _____ / _____
5. Is there a German restaurant in Islington? – _____ / _____
6. Sorry, I can't come to your party. – _____ / _____
7. Here's a German magazine. – _____ / _____
8. No, you can't play here. – _____ / _____
9. Let's go to the snack bar. – _____ / _____
10. This vindaloo – is it very hot? – _____ / _____

2 What have they got?

What can you say about these people and their things? Write the sentences down in your exercise book.

3 House crossword[1]

Across

2. It's for a car or a van.
4. An English living room has got a ... .
7. You can make music on it at home.
8. You can go up the ... or down the ... .
9. You can look out of the ... .
11. There's a big ... in the garden.
12. It's high up, under the roof.
14. The Bradens have got a ... of old things.
15. A lot of (11. across).
16. Go in the front door and you are in the ... .
17. The families' ... are all different.
19. "You say yes, I say ... !"
20. There's a (4. across) in the ... .
22. The Wilsons have got a ..., not a house.
24. How high is your house? – I don't ... .
25. There are nine ... in the Bradens' house.
26. They have got a house in London ..., but only for ten more weeks!
27. Their house isn't ... – it's old.

Down

1. There's a big ... in the kitchen.
2. There's a front and a back ... .
3. They are in the bedrooms.
4. There are trees and ... in the garden.
5. There are ... on the wall.
6. There's a snack for you in the ... .
10. Big families have got two ... .
13. There's a table with six ... .
18. The cat is on the ... in the living room.
20. Let's go out into the garden: we can play with the dog on the ... .
21. You can see it high up on a house; it can be red, or brown, or black.
23. "You say high, I say ... !"

[1] ['krɒswɜːd]

20 twenty

UNIT 3

1 School subjects

W	R	E	X	P	H	K	D	S	G	N	Y	P
D	C	M	E	R	I	J	F	R	E	N	C	H
K	G	A	M	E	S	L	W	V	O	X	E	E
I	U	T	D	S	T	C	T	I	G	W	B	A
Z	Q	H	V	X	O	D	E	N	R	F	H	L
M	U	S	I	C	R	S	D	R	A	M	A	T
D	F	H	M	E	Y	S	K	A	P	R	A	H
O	X	C	E	N	G	L	I	S	H	T	K	L
L	H	G	V	E	W	N	B	A	Y	E	Z	O
Y	S	C	I	E	N	C	E	C	X	U	I	V

→ _____
_____
_____
_____
_____

↓ _____
_____
_____
_____

2 Short for ...

ad — *advertisement*

CD — _____

N.Y. — _____

PE — _____

THU — _____

FRI — _____

SUN — _____

IS SHORT FOR

Monday — _____

electronic mail — _____

Wednesday — _____

Information Technology — _____

Tuesday — _____

Saturday — _____

3 Numbers

Listen and write the numbers.

1. ____ 3. ____ 5. ____ 7. ____ 9. ____ 11. ____ 13. ____ 15. ____
2. ____ 4. ____ 6. ____ 8. ____ 10. ____ 12. ____ 14. ____ 16. ____

4 Time by the clock

three o'clock · quarter to three · half past two · quarter past four · five o'clock

five past five · twenty-five past five · twenty-five to six · twenty to six · ten past six

5 What's the time?

1. seven o'clock
2. half past seven
3. quarter to eight
4. ten to eight
5. quarter past seven
6. five o'clock
7. quarter past five
8. five past six
9. twenty five to six
10. seven o'clock

6 Clocks and the time

Write down the time. Use your exercise book.

Example: It's ten past four. / It's four ten.

4:10	3:05	10:45
1:25	2:30	9:35
6:25	12:12	9:55
5:20	8:17	3:59

7 This / that – these / those   Put in the words.

1. This dog here is nice but that dog is not.
2. These people in the picture here are all friends of the school.
3. This bike is good but that bike over there is expensive.
4. That woman over there has got a very good job.
5. Those houses over there are very old.
6. This door here is for the pupils and that door over there is for the teachers.
7. The children are in these pictures and their parents are in those pictures over there.

1 School words

subjects
art

places
assembly hall

people
headteacher

things
timetable

2 Tarkan – a personal profile[1]

a) Complete the sentences.
b) Work with a partner. Ask and answer questions on Tarkan's profile. Use 'do', 'does', 'don't' and 'doesn't'.

1. _____ in Langenfeld with his family.
2. _____ on his bike.
3. _____ drum computer for 'The Good Vibes'.
4. His parents and sisters _____ his reggae music.
5. At school Tarkan _____ Maths and IT.
6. _____ homework in the kitchen.
7. _____ TV.
8. _____ for Neunkirchen football club.
9. Later he _____ in a big city.
10. And of course he _____ with computers.

[1] [ˌpɜːsnl ˈprəʊfaɪl] persönliche Kurzbiographie

3 Word order

Make sentences. Use your exercise book.

1. for long walks / Liz and Milly / can go
2. some questions / want to ask / the pupils
3. play hockey / they / at the weekends
4. has got / the band / great instruments
5. Maths / we / on Mondays / have got
6. usually / animals / vets / like
7. at 9 o'clock / she / goes to bed / always
8. at home / in the evenings / she is / usually
9. by bus / they / go / never / to school
10. on Sundays / often / works / Dr Modi

"Why do I want to do Art? Simple. They don't want me in Music, Drama, Chemistry, French, Biology, Technology or History."

4 A picture story: School dog

Write down the story with some sentences to go with the cartoons. Use your exercise book. To start you off:

Cartoon 1: A boy goes to school in the morning. He says goodbye …
Cartoon 2: But the dog wants … The boy doesn't …
Cartoon 3: At school the boy says, … and the dog …
Cartoon 4: When the boy opens his desk … All the other children …

5 Tandem[1] work

[1]['tændəm] [2][swɒp] *(aus)tauschen* [3][raɪd] *reiten, hier: fahren* [4][miːt] *treffen*

What do you often / sometimes / usually / always / never do after school? Swap[2] with a partner so that he / she can write an article about you and you about him / her.

	often	sometimes	usually	always	never	every weekend	on Saturdays
listen to music							
watch TV							
play with dog / cat							
work with computer							
ride[3] around on bike							
play computer games							
meet[4] friends							
do sports							
smoke							

STEP B

1 ... because ...

Look at the texts in your English book (pp. 46 / 47) and complete these sentences.

1. Stephanie does extra jobs because _____
2. James does most of the practical jobs in the house because _____
3. James wants to be a vet one day because _____
4. Joanna doesn't like the bullies because _____
5. And she hates one of the bullies because _____
6. Gina hates smoking because _____
7. Ben doesn't take drugs because _____
8. Ben hasn't got a girlfriend because _____

2 The people in Units 1-3

a) *Think of ten different people in your English book and write what they often, sometimes, usually, always, never do or don't do. Use your exercise book.*

Example: Dr Modi works as a vet. He often ...

b) *Now work with a partner. Ask and answer questions about the people in your lists. Use 'do', 'does' and 'don't', 'doesn't'.*

3 Words with y   *Say these words and then put them in the right list.*

| you | baby | hey | many | year | usually | way | assembly |
| key | my | stay | why | day | hobby | your | try | yes | say |

[j] _____

[ɪ] _____

[eɪ] _____

[aɪ] _____

4 The lost cat — by Shel Silverstein

All the lines of this poem are mixed up¹. Can you rewrite² the poem?

Does anyone know?

We don't know where she's at,

We can't find the cat,

Let's ask this walking hat³.

Oh, where did she go?

We can't _____

_____

_____

_____

_____ hat.

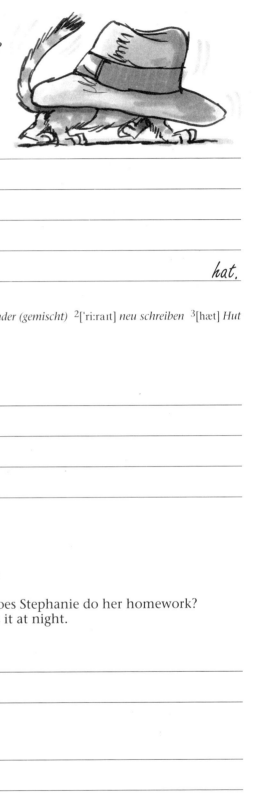

¹[ˌmɪksˈtʌp] *durcheinander (gemischt)*   ²[ˈriːraɪt] *neu schreiben*   ³[hæt] *Hut*

5 Word pairs

Find and write down the partner.

need _____   day _____

bet _____   right _____

swift _____   wait _____

Mr Bean _____   give _____

6 Stephanie

Write questions and answers.

1. Stephanie does her homework at … .

2. Stephanie's grandma gives her some … .

Example:

When does Stephanie do her homework?
She does it at night.

3. Stephanie wants to … … … … when she's 20.

4. Stephanie's best friend lives … … … .

5. Stephanie lives with her … … … .

| CHECK-IN | STEP A | STEP B | **STEP C** | TRACK | CHECK-OUT |

1 Verb puzzle

Find ten verbs. Use the verbs and write down ten sentences in your exercise book.

W	R	E	X	P	H	K	D	S	W	G	Y	P
D	C	M	E	R	I	J	F	E	A	T	C	H
K	W	O	R	K	S	L	W	V	T	Z	E	R
W	A	N	T	S	T	C	T	I	C	B	B	A
Z	L	H	V	X	O	P	E	C	H	A	S	E
M	K	S	I	C	R	L	F	R	E	R	A	X
U	S	E	M	E	W	A	I	T	S	K	A	H
O	X	C	E	N	G	Y	G	S	H	S	K	L
L	H	G	V	E	W	S	H	A	Y	E	Z	O
Y	S	C	N	E	N	C	T	C	X	U	I	V

➡ want, chase, wait, work, use

⬇ watch, walk, bark, fight, play

2 Time for fun

What time is it when an elephant[1] sits on your chair? _____

What kind[2] of phones do musicians[3] use? _____

Write down in English: Nach meiner Uhr ist es zwei vor zwei.

My clock says it's _____

Nach meiner Uhr ist es auch zwei vor zwei.

My clock says it's _____

[1] ['elıfənt] [2] [kaınd] *Art, Sorte* [3] [mjuː'zıʃn] *Musiker(in)*

3 A sick dog at Dr Modi's

There is a girl with her sick dog at Dr Modi's. *Listen and put in the words.*

Hello, young lady. Hello, little dog. What can I do for _____ ?   you   them

Come on, dog. What's wrong with _____ ?   her

Can't you tell _____ ? Well, let _____ see.   her   it

Can you put _____ on the table, please? Thank _____ .   you

What about dog biscuits[1]? Does she eat _____ ?   you   me

And water? Does she drink _____ ?   us

Well, I think, we can help _____ .

[1] ['bıskıt] *Keks*

1 The letter e — Sort the words.

1. You can't hear[1] the letter *e* as a sound.

   homework, like, smoke, hate, take, joke, house, chase, opposite, live

2. You can hear the letters *e, ee, ea* or *ie* as an [i:].

   eat, read, mean, he, she

3. You can hear the letter *e* as an [e].

   get, never, forget, help, best, next, spend, bet, pet

homework	eat
get	read
like	never
smoke	pet
forget	mean
hate	help
best	take
he	joke
next	house
spend	bet
chase	she
opposite	live

[1] [hɪə] hören

2 Double letters

Complete the words with double letters.

a____embly   sch___l   le___on   di___erent   aftern___n   we____

usua____y   ho____ies   f____tba____   te____y   g____d   cla____

vo____eyba____   w____k   si____y   bu____y   b____k   cart____n

3 Picture sentences

a) Can you write the words for these sentences?

I like cats.

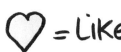

b) Make some more picture sentences for your friends.

[1] speak [spiːk] sprechen

1 Blacky

Complete the sentences.

1. Blacky works as a _____ _____ .

2. She and Mark Morton live in _____ _____ _____ .

3. The two are good _____ .

4. They make a _____ _____ .

5. Blacky wears a _____ _____ .

6. This is like a _____ for her.

7. At night she _____ _____ _____ _____ _____ _____ _____ .

8. Blacky must _____ Mark's commands.

9. These commands are: _____ , _____ , _____ , _____ , _____ and _____ .

10. Traffic lights are a problem because _____ _____ _____ .

11. You mustn't _____ a guide dog because that confuses them.

12. And you mustn't give a guide dog _____ _____ with loud noises.

2 Commands

Sometimes a dog does things wrong. Write down your commands to go with the cartoons.

| | CHECK-IN | STEP A | STEP B | STEP C | TRACK | **CHECK-OUT** |

1 The school alphabet

A	*assembly*	I	IT	R	room
B	book	J		S	science
C	class	K	kids	T	teacher
D	Drama	L	Lunch	U	uniform
E	english	M	Music, Maths	V	vacation
F	French	N	number	W	work
G	German	O		X	_____
H	History	P	pupils	Y	year
		Q	question	Z	_____

2 The odd one out

Write down the odd one out. The first letters of the words make a new word.

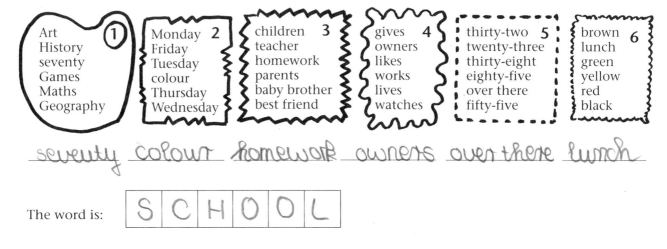

1. Art / History / seventy / Games / Maths / Geography
2. Monday / Friday / Tuesday / colour / Thursday / Wednesday
3. children / teacher / homework / parents / baby brother / best friend
4. gives / owners / likes / works / lives / watches
5. thirty-two / twenty-three / thirty-eight / eighty-five / over there / fifty-five
6. brown / lunch / green / yellow / red / black

seventy   colour   homework   owners   over there   lunch

The word is: | S | C | H | O | O | L |

3 My week

Write about your good or bad days. Use your exercise book.

Example: Monday is a good day for me because we've got Maths at school and I like it.
           Tuesday is … .   Go on.

4 An interview with some little green men

There's a UFO[1] in your back garden. Some little green men are in it. They are very friendly and they speak English. *What can you ask them? Write down ten questions. Your partner can give the answers. Take turns[2].*

Do you …   … watch TV?

        … read lots of comics?   … like cats?

    … listen to music?   … go to bed early?

            … play football?

[1][ˌjuːefˈəʊ] [2][ˌteɪk ˈtɜːnz] *sich abwechseln*

30 *thirty*

UNIT 4

1 A London crossword

➡

1. London's theatreland is in the ... End.
6.
7. You can watch this in a theatre.
8. Word for different forms of transport.
10.
11. If everybody knows about it, it is ... .
13. There is one inside Big Ben.
15. Opposite of 'slow'.
16. *Cats* and *Phantom of the Opera* are ... .
18.
20.
21. Opposite of 9. down.

⬇

2. Opposite of 'buy'.
3. Harrods is a ... .
4.
5.
7. The tourist takes a ... of the sights.
9. Things in London shops are often ... .
12. You can see the time on it.
14. When you sit and eat outside, you have a ... .
17.
19. You can see more from the ... of an 'official London sightseeing bus'.

1 At Covent Garden

Match the sentence parts and put in the missing words.

1. The man is walking on a bed of nails
2. The people are clapping
3. Jimmy's feet hurt
4. Maike is sitting on Liam's shoulders
5. The man is going around with a hat
6. Maike hasn't got much money with her
7. Liz isn't with Liam today

a) _____ Liam is standing on them.
b) _____ she can see what is happening.
c) _____ his feet don't hurt.
d) _____ she's having her piano lesson.
e) _____ they think the man is great.
f) _____ she isn't doing any shopping.
g) _____ not everyone is putting in money.

1. ____ 2. ____ 3. ____ 4. ____ 5. ____ 6. ____ 7. ____

2 Right or wrong?

a) *Are these sentences right or wrong?*

1. Two women are feeding the birds.
2. A girl is eating an ice cream.
3. Four boys are playing football.
4. A woman is writing a postcard.
5. A man is selling hot dogs.
6. A girl is singing.
7. Two men are listening to the song.
8. A family is having a picnic.
9. A dog is sleeping under a tree.
10. Two women are reading books.

right	wrong

b) *Correct¹ the wrong sentences. Use your exercise book.*

c) *What else is happening? Find five more things and write sentences.*

¹[kə'rekt] *korrigieren*

3 Questions and answers

[ˈɔːdə] *Reihenfolge*

Put the words in the right order[1] to make questions. Use your exercise book and answer the questions.

1. doing / are / what / you?
2. friend / you / with / are / working / a?
3. are / snack / eating / you / a?
4. classroom / you / sitting / are / your / in?
5. shoes / wearing / you / are?
6. your / teacher / what / doing / now / is?

1. _____
2. _____
3. _____
4. _____
5. _____
6. _____

4 What are they doing?

Put in the verbs in the correct form.

[ˈdaɪəri] *Tagebuch*

think – phone – write – do (2x) – run – go – collect
work – play – talk – sit – wait – sleep

1. _____ Liam and Sebastian _____ ?
   No, they _____ _____ computer games.

2. Why _____ Jimmy and Maike _____ ?
   They _____ _____ to a party, and they're late.

3. What _____ Mrs Braden _____ ?
   She _____ _____ money.

4. Who _____ you _____ to, Sandra?
   To my parents. They _____ _____ from Germany!

5. Why _____ you _____ here, Max?
   I _____ _____ for Nicola.

6. _____ you _____ , Tarkan?
   No, I _____ _____ !

7. _____ Tessa _____ her homework?

8. No, she _____ _____ her diary[1].

5 Tandem work

Work with a partner. One of you looks at role card A and the other at card B. Don't look at your partner's card.

A

a) *Ask your partner what these people are doing. Make notes of the answers.*

Mr Clifton
The Wilsons
Tarkan
Liz and Liam

Example: What is Tarkan doing?

b) *Answer your partner's questions about what these people are doing.*

Nicola
Mr Modi
Sebastian
Max

c) *With your partner, write eight sentences about what everyone is doing.*

B

a) *Answer your partner's questions about what these people are doing.*

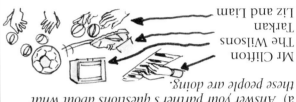

Mr Clifton
The Wilsons
Tarkan
Liz and Liam

b) *Ask your partner what these people are doing. Make notes of the answers.*

Example: I think he's playing football.

Nicola
Mr Modi
Sebastian
Max

c) *With your partner, write eight sentences about what everyone is doing.*

6 Seeing the sights

[1] ['daɪəlɒg] *Gespräch, Dialog*

Listen to the dialogues[1] and find the right picture for each dialogue. Make notes of keywords: they help you to find the right picture.

ROCK CIRCUS

SPEAKER'S CORNER

LONDON TRANSPORT MUSEUM

BUCKINGHAM PALACE

LONDON ZOO

Dialogue	Keywords	Picture
1		
2		
3		
4		
5		

1 The bank robbers

Put the parts of the text in the right order.

A Julie's car comes round the corner. "Come on, Joe," says Harry. "Don't worry – I've got the bag. Quick!"

B Julie stops the car. "Get out, Joe." she says. "Find the girl and bring back the money. All of it. And don't move, Harry. You're staying with me."

C "Of course!" says Joe. "You've got the bag, Harry. See how much is inside the box!"

D "You idiot!" Joe says to Maike. He stands up, but his head hurts. Everything is going around in circles.

E but there is no box, no money and no gold. Harry looks at Joe and tries to speak. "B-B-But ... Where ...? Who ...? I don't understand!"

F Joe gets out of the car. Good – he can still see the girl and her friend. They're going into Bank tube station.

G "What's going on?" asks Julie. "Tell me this is a joke, please!" Then Joe remembers: "You've got the wrong bag, Harry! The girl has got our money!"

H They run to the car and jump inside. "Have you got the money?" Julie asks them.

I Harry opens the bag. He takes out a map of London, two sightseeing guides, some postcards of Big Ben and half a cheese[1] sandwich,

[1] ['tʃiːz] *Käse*

1. ____ 2. ____ 3. ____ 4. ____ 5. ____ 6. ____ 7. ____ 8. ____ 9. ____

2 A summary[1]

is hiding – is following – pulls – close – are taking – leaves
looks – get (4x) – want – is talking – says – finds – sees (2x)
dials – has got – jump – opens – are walking – gets (2x)

Put in the verbs.

[1] ['sʌmri] *Zusammenfassung*

At the Tower of London Maike _____ a man with red hair. He _____ like the man in the City. Maike and Jimmy _____ to go to the London Aquarium, so they _____ onto the Circle Line. The man with the red hair is on the train. He _____ behind a newspaper. Jimmy and Maike _____ out after four stops, but the man _____ out too. He _____ to someone on his mobile phone. Jimmy and Maike _____ along the river when Maike _____ the car from the City. The car _____ them. The man _____ out, but Jimmy _____ a plan. He _____ in a loud voice that they _____ the train to Victoria. They _____ in the train, with the man behind them. But before the doors _____ , they _____ out again. The train _____ the station, with the man inside, and Jimmy and Maike _____ into a train to Brixton. Maike _____ her bag and _____ not her maps and guide books, but a box full of money. Jimmy _____ a mobile phone out of his pocket and _____ 999.

1 What is where?

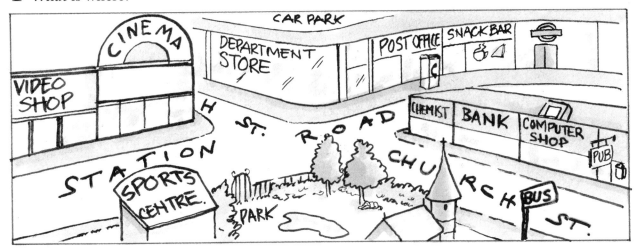

What are the prepositions and adverbs in the box? Use them to complete the sentences.

| no het felt fo | xent ot | idbhen | spootipe | ni tronf fo |
| no het ronecr fo | | teenweb | drune | |

1. The bank is _____ the chemist and the computer shop.

2. The department store is _____ Station Road and Church Street.

3. The Odeon Cinema is _____ the department store.

4. There is a bus stop _____ the computer shop.

5. _____ the department store there is a car park.

6. A dog is sleeping _____ the tree.

7. The snack bar is _____ the post office.

8. The computer shop is _____ the pub.

2 Excuse me, please

Three people ask you the way. Use the picture in exercise 1 and answer their questions.

1. You are waiting at the bus stop.

   Excuse me, please. Is there a telephone around here?

2. You are coming out of the tube station.

   Excuse me. Can you tell me the way to the sports centre?

3. You are outside the video shop.

   Excuse me, please. Where is St. Mary's Church?

3 At the ticket office

A tourist from Italy[1] is buying tickets for the museum[2] Madame Tussauds[3].

Woman: Four tickets, please.
Man: That's two hundred pounds, madam.
Woman: Two hundred pounds? That can't be right! It says here that tickets are ten pounds for adults[4].
Man: But ... don't you want tickets for kids?
Woman: No! We're adults!
Man: Not forty?

a) *Complete the sentences.*

1. The woman wants to buy tickets for _____ _____ .

2. The man thinks she wants to buy tickets for _____ _____ .

b) *Listen and tick (✓) the sentence you hear[5].*

1. Sixty kids.	☐	Six tickets.	☐
2. Thirteen tickets.	☐	Thirty tickets.	☐
3. I'm hungry.	☐	I'm angry.	☐
4. That's my food!	☐	That's my foot!	☐
5. My head is hot.	☐	My hat is hot.	☐
6. Give me the right book.	☐	Give me the white book.	☐
7. Can't you see the funny side[6]?	☐	Can't you see the funny sight?	☐
8. I want to walk.	☐	I want to work.	☐

[1]['ɪtli] [2][mjuːˈziːəm] [3]['mædəm tʊˈsɔːdz] [4]['ædʌlt] *Erwachsene(r)* [5][hɪə] *hören* [6][saɪd] *Seite*

4 Verb snake

The 23 verbs on the right are hiding in this verb snake[1]. Can you find them?

L→	I→	S	E	A	V	E	N	K	P
N←	E←	T↓	L	W	O	D	I	T	U
S↓	A	I	T	R	L	O	H	M	A
I	W	E	U	I	L	W	T	E	K
N	G	S	G	T	O	F	E	C	O
Y	A	S	E	E	C	O	M	L	L
C	L	R	K	A	T	L	A	E	C
H	P	E	Y	H	I	D	I	D	T
E	D	A	R	R	O	E	E	S	P
C	K	A	S	K	W	S	E	T	O

worry wait
play think sing
make dial
leave take come
check guess see
read collect stop
hide do ask
follow write
put listen

[1][sneɪk] *Schlange*

1 Where is the leaf[1]?

In your exercise book, write where the leaf is now, or where it is going.

Example: In picture 1 the leaf is flying around the traffic lights.

| in | under | through | at the end of | on | behind | over | around |

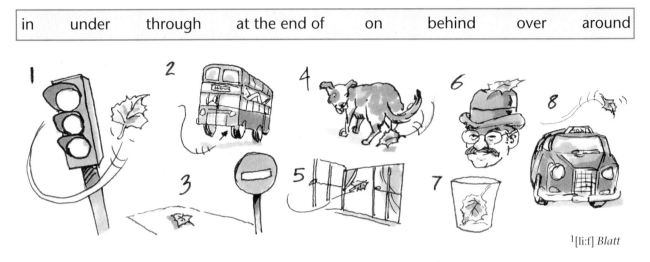

[1] [liːf] *Blatt*

2 A guide to London

Put in the headings from the guide.   [1][əˌkɒməˈdeɪʃn] *Unterkunft*   [2][trɪp] *Ausflug*   [3][ɪntrəˈdʌkʃn] *Einführung*

Comedy – Dance – Business – Accommodation[1] – Getting around – Museums
London by Season – Restaurants – Galleries – Trips[2] out of Town – Students
Music: Rock, Folk and Jazz – Theatre – Information – Sightseeing – Film
Cafés and Brasseries – After Hours – Children – Women – Pubs and Bars
Sport and Fitness – Music: Classical and Opera – Introduction[3]

From *Time Out – London Guide* (http://www.timeout.co.uk/TO/London Guide)

1 The same sound

a) *Put the words in pairs of the same sound. Add a third word if you can.*

you	key	straight	right	break
more	road	where	head	street
	read	gone		phone

feed	their	through	wait	door
code	bed	own	make	write
	eat	tree	on	

you — through, key —

b) *In your exercise book, write sentences with five of the pairs (or groups of three).*

Example: Why are **you** looking **through** the window?

2 A postcard from your home town

Imagine a tourist in your home town[1] is writing a postcard to a friend. Use an extra piece of paper, draw a picture of a famous or interesting sight in your town (or take a photo). Write the text on the other side. You can write about …

- … where you are, and what it's like.
- … the weather.
- … the people.
- … what you think of the town.
- … the picture on the other side of the postcard.
- … what you're doing at the moment.
- … what you want to do tomorrow.
- …

[1] ['həʊmˌtaʊn] Heimatstadt

3 Weather words

Put in words for a weather mind map.

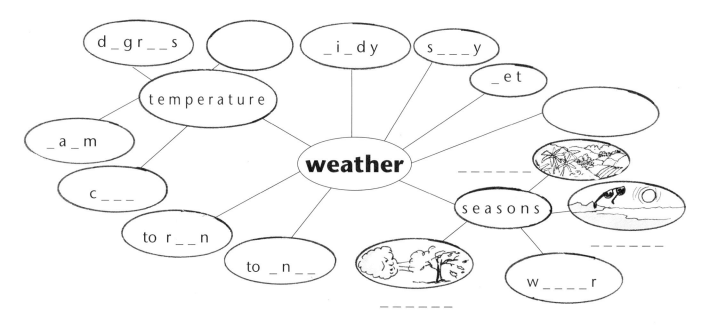

1 Verbs, nouns and prepositions

Match the words and pictures in A, B and C, and put in the prepositions and nouns in B.

A	B	C
1. stop	a number ____ a _____	
2. dial	the way ____ a _____	
3. open	_at_ a red _traffic light_	
4. see	____ a bed _____	
5. walk	____ the top ____ a _____	
6. find	the time ____ the _____	
7. sit	the door _____ a _____	

2 What are they doing?

Look at the pictures on pages 58 and 59 in your English book. Write what people are doing.

1. On page 58 a little girl _____

2. A man at the tube station _____

3. The people at Trafalgar Square _____

4. Tourists in the West End _____

5. On page 59 some men _____

6. At Hampstead Heath a man and a woman _____

7. People in Harrods _____

3 Questions and answers   *Write questions and answers.*

1. *Is Sandra playing tennis? — Yes, she is.*
2. *Are Jimmy and Maike running? — No,* _____

40 *forty*

UNIT 5

1 Shops

Look at the pictures. Write down in your exercise book what kind of shop it is, and what you can get there. Give two or three things for each shop. Start: A is a ... You can get ... there.

| CHECK-IN | **STEP A** | STEP B | STEP C | TRACK | CHECK-OUT |

1 Asking for things

¹['speʃl] *besonders, speziell* ²[paʊnd] *Pfund (auch Gewicht)* ³['pækɪt] *Packung, Schachtel*

You must ask for some things in a special¹ way.
Use the words on the right.

glass   pound²   packet³   bag   box   pair

A pound of bananas, please.

2 How much or how many?

What is the right question?

1. _____ is a pair of Doc Martens shoes?
2. _____ CDs are there in the box?
3. _____ is this calendar?
4. _____ of these postcards have you got?
5. _____ computer games have you got?
6. _____ is this old comic?
7. _____ is the ice cream?
8. _____ books about astronomy have you got?

| CHECK-IN | **STEP A** | STEP B | STEP C | TRACK | CHECK-OUT |

3 Do you like ...? Would you like ...?

Yes, I do. / No, I don't.   I like ... / I don't like ...
Good idea!   Yes, please. / I'd like a ..., please. / No, thanks.

a) *Answer the questions.*

[1][mɪlk] *Milch* [2][kʌp] *Tasse* [3]['ʃʊgə] *Zucker*

Do you like ice cream? _____

Which do you like best – vanilla or chocolate? _____

I like banana. What about you? _____

Would you like an ice cream now? _____

Would you like something to drink too? _____

Let me see. They've only got milk[1] or water. Hm ... some people don't like milk. What about you?
_____

Or would you like to go to the café over there? _____

b) *Now ask the questions.*

_____ ? No, I don't like coffee, I only like tea.

_____ ? Yes, a cup[2] of tea, please.

_____ ? Just a little milk, please. But no sugar[3].

_____ ?

Black Forest gateau? Isn't that *Schwarzwälder Kirschtorte* ? Oh, yes, I like it very much.

_____ ? No, thanks. I'm not hungry enough now.

4 More market dialogues

Put in the right words. If there's a picture, it's the name of the thing or things. If there's no picture, it's 'some' or 'any' or 'a / an'.

1 – Have you got _____ really nice _____ ?

– Well, we've got _____ American ones here. They're very good, so they're a bit more

expensive. Are you looking for _____ special colour?

– Oh, _____ nice, happy colour, I think. Like red or yellow.

– There aren't _____ yellow ones, but ... yes, there are _____ very nice red ones.

Take a look. And what about _____ nice yellow _____ to go with it?

– Oh, no, thanks. I don't need _____ of those. I've got enough _____

at home.

2 – Excuse me. There are _____ big _____ up there, but I can't see

inside. Can you tell me what's in them?

– Well, there are _____ more silver things in that _____ , and in the other

one there are _____ old English _____ a bit like that green

_____ over there. Would you like to look? I can get them down for you.

– Oh, no, I can't carry _____ things like that back to Germany! Hmmm ... but maybe

_____ old silver _____ for my mother ...

– Sure thing! There are _____ very nice old _____ there. Here,

take a look at this one.

STEP B

1 What Sebastian thinks

Check how well you understand the story. Put what Sebastian thinks in the right order. Write in the numbers 1-5.

2 What the store detectives see

Put in the right words.

English	German	string	prices	teapot	a bit	room
voice	mistake	problem	computer	around	pocket	door
table	scene	sorry	souvenirs	watch	meet	understand
TV	street	pulls	shows	checks	department	nothing
everything	model	laughing	carrying	behind	away	still

A store detective is standing at the door of a _____ store in Tottenham Court Road. She sees two kids in the _____ , a boy and a girl. They are speaking _____ . "They are shopping for _____ ," she thinks, because they are _____ a lot of things. As they come into the store, they _____ another boy. They start talking to him in _____ . Then they walk into the store. They are talking and _____ . But the German boy looks _____ nervous[1] as he talks about how terrible the _____ are in the store. The detective thinks she must _____ these kids, so she goes into a room where she can see _____ in the store on _____ .

The kids go up to the computer games _____ . The German boy looks _____ . But the girl first _____ the English boy what she has got: a funny _____ and a teddybear. She _____ a _____ on the teddybear, and it sings a song in a silly _____ . She also shows him a _____ of Big Ben, but looks over to her friend as she talks about it. The they go over to him and stand _____ him. But the detectives can see what he does with the game in his hand: he puts it in his _____ !

Then the kids start to walk _____ . The detectives can _____ see them, but they can't hear them any more.

They go down to the _____ , and when the kids get there, the detectives ask them to come into a small _____ . The English boy says the detectives are making a big _____ . But he knows they've got a real _____ when he sees the _____ on video! They put all their things on the _____ . The detectives can't _____ why they can't find the CD. The man _____ their pockets. But there's _____ there. They must let the kids go. The man says he's _____ .

[1][nɜːvəs]

3 The last concert

[1]['hedeɪk] Kopfweh [2][fluː] Grippe [3][wɪ'ðaʊt] ohne [4]['keə] es macht uns nichts aus

Do you remember Liz and Liam's birthday party? Sebastian doesn't go to it because he has a headache[1]. Well, he says he has a headache, and everybody believes him. But the next day, the day of the band's last concert, his friends are not so sure ... a) *Put the sentences in the right places in the picture story.*

Sorry I'm late, guys!

Everything seems to be OK now. But where's Sebastian?   Maybe he's got the flu[2].

Why isn't he with you, Kevin? We can't play without[3] our electric guitar!

Is Liam there, Mrs Braden?   Don't be silly – only Sandra and I know, and we don't care[4].

Come on, Sebastian – everybody's waiting for you! The concert is at 5.30!

Tell them I can't come. I've got a headache!   OK, I can try. But he can't be as silly as that!

And it's a bit strange: a headache yesterday, OK all the morning, and now a headache again?

Hm ... I think I know what's wrong with him. And it isn't the flu.

⟨b⟩ *Now tell the story. Write it in your exercise book. You can start like this:*

It's the day of their last concert. Sebastian is ... Kevin comes ... and says, "...," but ...

1 More of the song

It's not easy to understand all the words of the song *In Camden Town*. There are a lot of words, and Suggs sings very fast! But we think we can help you to understand some more ...
Listen again, and try to complete the words of verses 2 and 3.

2. A drunken busker[1] hits the pavement[2], sending _____ in the air,

   Towards[3] a broken-down[4] _____ full of people going nowhere.

   A string[5] of Irish pubs[6] as far as you can _____ ,

   Greek[7], Indian, Chinese. Or _____ a cup of tea?

   There's tapas, fracas, alcohol, tobaccos,

   Bongs, bonga binga, Portuguese maracas,

   There's reggae in the jeggae, music everywhere,

   Every kind of song and dance, madness[8] in the air!

Don't worry what all these words mean!

[1][ˌdrʌŋkn ˈbʌskə] *besoffener Straßenmusikant*
[2][ˈpeɪvmənt] *Bürgersteig*
[3][təˈwɔːdz] *in Richtung, gegen*
[4][ˌbrəʊknˈdaʊn] *kaputt, Pannen-*
[5][strɪŋ] *hier: Reihe*
[6][pʌb] *Kneipe*
[7][griːk] *griechisch*
[8][ˈmædnɪs] *Wahnsinn*

Chorus:

In Camden Town, I'll meet you by the Underground,

In Camden Town, we'll walk there as the sun goes down,

In Camden Town –

In Camden Town you can do anything you want to (do).

The _____ say – ooh ooh ooh ooh,

They _____ – ooh ooh ooh ooh,

Sing up! – ooh ooh ooh ooh,

What's my name? An invisible[9] game! – ooh ooh ooh ooh.

3. The two fat Americans[10] interrupt[11] their stay[12],

   They put down their _____ , they were clamped and towed away[13],

   There's _____ cakes[14], designer fakes[15], fathers dressed as nuns[16],

   _____ kind of _____ here, the night has just begun[17].

Chorus: In Camden Town ...

[9][ɪnˈvɪsɪbl] *unsichtbar*
[10][ˌfæt_əˈmerɪkənz] *dicke Amerikaner(innen)*
[11][ˌɪntəˈrʌpt] *unterbrechen*
[12][steɪ] *Aufenthalt*
[13][ˈklæmpt_ən_ˌtəʊd_əˈweɪ] *(Auto) wurde festgeklemmt und abgeschleppt*
[14][keɪk] *Kuchen*
[15][feɪk] *gefälschter Designer-artikel*
[16][ˌdrest_əz_ˈnʌnz] *als Nonnen verkleidet*
[17][bɪˈgʌn] *hat gerade angefangen*

If you need more help, you can read these words the other way around!

| cisum | yreve | hsikruT | sgab | gnis | stsiruot |
| ekil uoy dluow | | ees | sub | | sgod toh |

1 Regular and irregular verbs

Put the verbs on the right into two lists, one for regular and one for irregular verbs. Give the basic[1] form of the verb.

played	came	happened	won	saw
bought	put	was / were	had	wanted
did	took	showed	laughed	thought
knew	met	said	went	told

regular	irregular

[1] ['beɪsɪk] Grund-

2 In the country shop

In the city, you must go to a different shop for different things – or to a big department store. In the country, some small shops have nearly everything! *Look at this picture of a country shop, and imagine[1] you were there last summer. There were four people in your group and each of you did something there. Tell the story.*

You can use these verbs – but in the past tense!

I / we all
mother
father
sister
brother
friend

buy		eat
get	play	read
have		like
change		find

a) *First write what you did.*

[1] [ɪˈmædʒɪn] sich vorstellen

I _____

My _____

_____

_____

b) *But maybe you didn't find what you wanted there? Or maybe some things weren't so good. Now write what you didn't find / like / do, etc. in the country shop.*

_____

_____

3 Sebastian's diary

While he was in London, Sebastian wrote his diary in English. Of course, he wrote about what happened, and what he did, in the past tense. a) *Put in the verbs in the right form.*

<u>Saturday, 23rd October</u>

Liam is a computer freak, just like me! Today he _____ me to a great computer store where you can try out all the games. We _____ great fun! I _____ the London Marathon one best. We _____ it four times, and I _____ very good at it. I _____ three times! Liam said, "Good for you, Sebastian!" – but I _____ he _____ happy about it. I _____ see from his face!

take
have
like   play
be   win
know   not be
can

<u>Sunday, 24th October</u>

I'm counting¹ my money because I'd like to buy that computer game – I _____ it again in an ad in one of the Sunday newspapers. No way! I just haven't got enough! I _____ Sandra to lend² me some money, but she _____ she _____ very little after yesterday – she _____ at the antiques market and _____ lots of silly old things! And she still _____ to buy some souvenirs for her mum and dad. Yes, she is silly!

see
ask
say   have
be   buy
want

<u>Monday, 25th October</u>

I _____ a very silly thing today. I _____ in town with Sandra, and we _____ to that computer store with the great games. I _____ that London Marathon game very much – and I _____ how to get it, money or no money. But we _____ Liam at the door, and I _____ – well, no chance³ today! But then Sandra _____ him all her souvenirs – really silly things! – and they _____ a lot about them. I _____ my chance, and _____ over to the games. I _____ what I _____, _____ it, and _____ it in my pocket. But Liam _____ what I _____. Sandra _____, "Put it back!" – and in the end I _____ OK, and _____ it back. But that _____ the end of the story! At the door there _____ two

do   be
come   want
know
meet   think
show
laugh   take
go   see
want   take   put
see   do   say
say   put
not be be

b) As Sebastian wrote, '… that wasn't the end of the story!' His diary goes on on the next page. What does he write? What happened next? Try to tell the rest of the story as Sebastian saw it – in the past tense, of course. Use your exercise book.

¹[kaʊnt] zählen ²[lend] (aus-)leihen ³[tʃɑːns] Chance, (gute) Gelegenheit

4 Ten days in New York

Here are some of the Braden family's plans for a trip to New York – and you can see what they really did. *Write a sentence for each plan.*

Start: On ... they ... / wanted to ... but ... / didn't ... , because ... . They ... ... instead[1].

April

[1][ɪnˈsted] *stattdessen* [2]= Statue of Liberty [ˈstætʃuː əv ˈlɪbəti] *Freiheitsstatue* [3][ˌelɪs ˈaɪlənd] *Museum in der Nähe von New York City* [4]= World Trade Center [ˌwɜːld ˈtreɪd ˌsentə] *Welthandelszentrum* [5][ˌempaɪə ˈsteɪt ˌbɪldɪŋ] *berühmtes Hochhaus in New York* [6][zuː] [7]*ausschlafen* [8][ˈdʒet læg] *Auswirkung der Zeitverschiebung*

Sat	01	pick up plane tickets ✓
Sun	02	pack bags ✓
Mon	03	get dollars from bank ✓
Tue	04	
Wed	05	fly to New York ✓
Thu	06	do sightseeing trip RAIN!
Fri	07	go shopping. 5th Ave.
Sat	08	Ellis Island[3] ✓
Sun	09	take boat to St. of Lib.[2]
Mon	10	Empire State Building[5] ✓
Tue	11	go up World Trade Ct.[4]
Wed	12	
Thu	13	visit zoo[6] ✓
Fri	14	do more shopping ✓
Sat	15	fly home ✓
Sun	16	sleep off[7] our jet lag![8] ✓

5 And what about you?

Imagine you were in New York last summer, and went shopping there. Write what you bought / didn't buy. Write about all the things in the pictures and use 'some' / 'any' where you need them. If you didn't buy any of these things, say why (didn't find / want ... , etc.). Use your exercise book.

1 Answers

What can you say? Find one good answer for each of these questions.

1. How much are these T-shirts, please? _____
2. Have you got a size S in this colour? _____
3. What colour do you want? _____
4. Excuse me, have you got any big postcards? _____
5. £7? That's too much! Can I have it for £5? _____
6. Where can I find a good London guide book? _____
7. How can I get from Islington to Camden? _____
8. What did you buy at the market? _____
9. Why didn't you buy anything at Harrods? _____
10. How did you get from Harrods back to Covent Garden? _____
11. What kind of ice cream would you like? _____
12. Sorry, the vanilla's all gone. What about chocolate or banana? _____

2 What can you get there?

Do you know what you can get in the different departments of a department store? (Use a dictionary.)

1. In one department, you can get CDs, records, music cassettes and … .
2. In another department, you can get boots and … .
3. Upstairs they sell … , modems, games and other software.
4. On the second floor, they have things like gloves, hats and … .
5. Downstairs they've got tables, … , sofas, cupboards, etc.
6. There are three departments for … : one each for men's, women's, and children's.
7. On the top floor, there are musical … .
8. There's lots of nice gold and silver … in this department.
9. Here you can find books, postcards, … , magazines and newspapers.
10. There's also a department for clocks and … .
11. Downstairs you can also get things for the kitchen, like knives and … .
12. Bags and other … things are also on the second floor.
13. If you're hungry, go to the … department on the first floor. You can get pet … there too!
14. You need some tennis balls? The … department is on the fourth floor.
15. You can get chocolates and other … near the door. They've got some very good ones!

3 A London and New York quiz

Write down:	London	New York
1. a famous sight		
2. a department store		
3. another shop		
4. a district		
5. a street		
6. a market		
7. a typical[1] snack		
8. a place for a snack		
9. the money		
10. the city transport system[2]		
11. a typical kind of music		
12. what you'd like to buy		

[1]['tɪpɪkl] *typisch* [2]['sɪstəm] *System*

4 Do you know what the pictures are?

a) *Look at the pictures, then write down what you know about them.*

1. _____
2. _____
3. _____
4. _____
5. _____

b) *Now imagine you were at one of these places. Write a short story about what you did there – and what you didn't do there. Use your exercise book.*

50 *fifty*

UNIT 6

1 Braintrainer[1]

The first rhymes[2] with why and it's also in why.
The second and thirteenth is in eyes[3] and in ice.
The third, fourth and eleventh are in wall, hill and Milly.
The fifth rhymes with snow and with no, but not now.
The sixth is in where, but it isn't in here.
The seventh is in scarf and in laugh and in half.
The eighth is in new, but it isn't in view.
The ninth is in wood and it's in good food too.
The tenth is in bridge, but it's not in the fridge.
The twelfth is in you and it rhymes with you too.

1		7		10	
2		8		11	
3		9		12	
4				13	
5					
6					

[1] ['breɪnˌtreɪnə] Gedächtnistrainer
[2] [raɪm] (sich) reimen [3] [aɪ] Auge

The letters make the words for Liz Braden's f _____ c _____ .

2 Mad Mrs Minns

a) Listen to Mrs Minns and put a tick (√) for the things she likes, and a cross (x) for the things she doesn't like.

b) Listen again and write down the adjectives Mrs Minns uses.

	☺	☹	adjectives
the bus service			
the weather today			
Liam's walls			
her sister's van			
tea			
coffee			
e-mail			
computer games			

3 One word from two

Make new words from two words, and complete the sentences.

1. Liz and Liam still haven't got their school _____ .
2. I'm sorry, but I don't _____ you.
3. Liam wants to paint his _____ walls.
4. Milly wants to go _____ with Liz.
5. Liam is wearing his new _____ .
6. There is snow here, there and _____ .
7. Mrs Braden is fixing the heating _____ .

stand
room   where
stairs   every
table   down   time
shirt   out
sweat   under
bed   side

4 Clothes

You'd like to buy eight of the things in the shop window. Write down in your exercise book what you say to the shop assistant[1] and work out how much you must pay[2].

Example: Excuse me, I'd like the pair of socks for £3.99.   Go on.

I'd like a ..., please.   Could I have those ...?   Excuse me, I'd like a pair of ...
Could I have the ...   I'd like those ...

[1] [ˈʃɒpəˌsɪstnt] *Verkäufer(in)*   [2] [peɪ] *(be)zahlen*

5 Getting ready for the school play

Pupils in the Drama Club at Penryn College are trying on clothes for a school play. Write what they say in the speech bubbles[1].

These are too small.   This is much too short.   These aren't long enough.
This isn't big enough.   These are too long.   These are too big.
This is too old.   These look like new.   This is too big.

[1] [ˈspiːtʃˌbʌbl] *Sprechblase*

1 The new start   *Put in the verbs.*

am   is   are   do   don't   does   doesn't

1. Liz and Liam _____ wearing their new school uniform.
2. Liz _____ like the colour of her skirt. She hates it!
3. Pupils in Year 8 _____ have assembly every morning.
4. When _____ assembly start?
5. Please be quiet. I _____ trying to work.
6. What _____ the teachers do in the staffroom?
7. Pete's friend is in the drama group. He _____ rehearsing for the school play.

The library at Penryn College

2 Red Nose Day

[1][æk'tɪvəti]   [2]['lɪsnə] *Hörer(in)*   [3]['dɜːti] *schmutzig*   [4]['speʃl] *speziell(e/r)*
[5]['fælməθ] *Hafenstadt in Cornwall*   [6]['laɪfbəʊt] *Rettungsboot*

A reporter is visiting Penryn College. *Choose the right words.*

Reporter: Hello, this is Pam Tucker at Radio Penryn. Well, it's Red Nose Day today, and people all over Britain _____ (wear / are wearing) red noses. I _____ (talk / am talking) to you now from Penryn College, and the pupils here _____ (have / are having) a lot of fun. So let's find out what they _____ (do / are doing). Hello, what's your name?

Pete: Pete. Hi!

Reporter: Tell me, Pete, _____ always _____ (do you wear / are you wearing) those silly pink trousers to school?

Pete: Of course I _____ (don't / am not)! We usually _____ (wear / are wearing) our boring school uniform, but on Red Nose Day we can wear what we want. Sometimes people _____ (give / are giving) us money for it!

Reporter: Great! So _____ (do you do / are you doing) this every year?

Pete: Yes, we _____ (do / are). And this time we _____ (try / are trying) something new. As you can see, we _____ (all do / are all doing) different activities[1] today.

Reporter: Tell our listeners[2] what _____ (you do / are doing) at the moment, Pete.

Pete: We _____ (wash / are washing) our teachers' cars.

Reporter: They're very dirty[3], I must say.

Pete: Yes. Some teachers _____ (never wash / are never washing) their cars, but they're happy to give us money to do it!

Reporter: Is the money for a special[4] charity?

Pete: Yes. Usually _____ (we give / are giving) all the money to the school, but this time we _____ (collect / are collecting) it for the Falmouth[5] Lifeboats[6].

| CHECK-IN | **STEP A** | STEP B | STEP C | TRACK | CHECK-OUT |

3 Sandra's questions

what   who   where   when   how often   why

Liz is talking to Sandra on the phone about her new home, but Sandra can't hear every word. *Write Sandra's question, and then give a possible answer for Liz.*

Example:

Liz: I'm painting my ...
Sandra: What are you painting?
Liz: A picture of Milly in the snow.

1. I'm painting my ...
2. Liam likes a ... in our class.
3. Mum is fixing the ...
4. Dad goes to ... on Fridays.
5. Mrs Minns comes once[1] a ...

6. Liam is wearing his new ...
7. Liam doesn't like snow because ...
8. We start at our new school on ...
9. ... is trying to eat my biscuits[2]!
10. I'm sitting in the ...

[1][wʌns] *einmal*
[2]['bɪskɪt] *Keks*

4 Opposites

Put in the opposites. You can find them on pages 92 and 93 of your English book.

1. quiet _____
2. over _____
3. starting _____
4. fun _____

4. buy _____
5. inside _____
6. early _____
7. wrong _____

9. old _____
10. always _____
11. go to sleep _____
12. fire _____

5 Present progressive or simple present?

Put in the verbs in the right form.

try   do   wear
buy   snow   make
rain   give   drink
play (2x)   take
sleep   choose   watch

1. *Liam:* What _____ you _____ , Liz?

   Liz: I _____ a cup[1] of coffee for Mrs Minns.

   Liam: Coffee? But Mrs Minns always _____ tea!

2. *Liam:* _____ it still _____ ?

   Pete: No, it _____ like crazy. Look – everything is white outside!

3. *Sandra:* _____ you _____ your school uniform, Liz?

   Liz: No, not at the moment. I _____ on some clothes for Red Nose Day!

   Sandra: Who _____ your clothes for you, Liz. You or your parents?

   Liz: My parents _____ me the money, but I _____ what I buy.

4. *Mr Braden:* Where is Liam? Is he _____ computer games again?

   Mrs Braden: No. I think he _____ Milly for a walk.

   Mr Braden: No, he isn't. Milly is here. She _____ in her basket[2].

5. *Mrs Wilson:* I can hear music. Is Maike _____ the piano?

   Mr Wilson: No. She and Jimmy _____ TV.

[1][kʌp] *Tasse* [2]['bɑːskɪt] *Korb*

1 Strange[1] noises

[1][streɪndʒ] *befremdlich, merkwürdig* [2]['emptɪ] *leer*

a) Mrs Minns is telling a story. *Listen and put the pictures in the right order.*

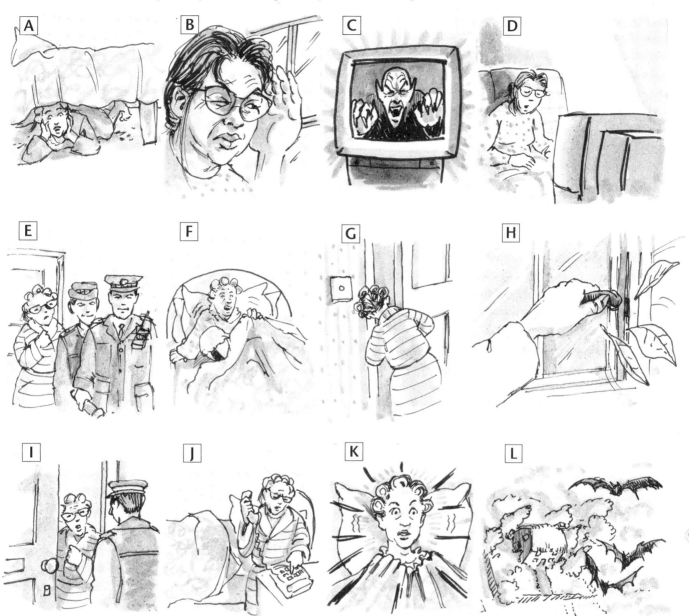

1. ___ 2. ___ 3. ___ 4. ___ 5. ___ 6. ___ 7. ___ 8. ___ 9. ___ 10. ___ 11. ___ 12. ___

b) *Write the story in your exercise book. Use the notes to help you.*

police laugh because – helpless – cat / dog? – go upstairs – dial 999 – get back into bed

open bedroom door – empty[2] house – woods – dark – quiet – TV – nothing interesting

tired – early night – police come – close windows – open living room door – get into bed

look out of window – can't move – Edgecombe – more noises – nothing there

Arthur gone – close window – windy – get up – hear voices – hide under bed

go downstairs – open front door – room very cold – strange noise

2 Getting ready for school

Put in the prepositions.

on (2x)   up (2x)   away   off   for (2x)   at   after

1. *Mr Braden:* Wake _____ Liam! It's 7.30 am.
2. *Mrs Braden:* Hurry _____ , Liz! What are you doing?
3. *Liz:* I'm looking _____ my pencil case. I can't find it!
4. *Liam:* Look _____ the snow! We can't go to school in this weather!
5. *Mr Braden:* I can drive you to school. Mum can stay and look _____ Milly.
6. *Mrs Braden:* Put _____ your scarf, Liz. It's cold outside.
7. *Mr Braden:* And take _____ your baseball cap, Liam. You can't wear that to school.
8. *Liam:* Come _____ Liz. Let's go.
9. *Liz:* Don't run _____ , Liam! Wait _____ me!

3 How do we get out?

Describe in your exercise book how to get from the castle to the boat. Use the verbs and the prepositions.

Example: First get out of the box. Then go into the ... . After that ...   *Go on.*

go   climb   get   jump | up   around   over   through   down   out   under

1 Classroom language

Your _____ (cheater) writes _____ (dwors) on the _____ (blodbarack) with a _____ (cipee) of _____ (klach), and then _____ (eshaws) it with a _____ (pensog). You can do your _____ (whekroom) in your _____ (ceesirex kobo). If you use a _____ (lipnec), you also need a _____ (lipnec rashpreen). If you make a _____ (timesak), you can use a _____ (beburr) and try again. You can also write with a _____ (nep) or a _____ (riob). If you can't draw straight[1] lines, use a _____ (lerur). You can put all these things in a _____ (lipnec eacs). You can look up a _____ (dwor) in a _____ (traindicoy). You can save your _____ (stone) in a _____ (fedrol). You can use a _____ (rapi) of _____ (scrossis) to _____ (tuc) things.

[1][streɪt] *gerade*

2 Questions and answers

Put the words in the right order to make short dialogues. Put in commas where you need to.

1. A: scissors/you/pair/have/a/of/got?   B: haven't/afraid/I'm/I
   A: _____   B: _____

2. A: may/your/borrow/please/I/dictionary?   B: is/the/using/moment/but/sorry/Pete/it/at
   A: _____   B: _____

3. A: biro/your/you/me/lend/can?   B: are/here/you/yes
   A: _____   B: _____

3 School jokes

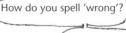
How do you spell 'wrong'?

That's wrong.

Good, I've got it right, then!
R-O-N-G.

Match the questions and answers.

1. Do you know how to spell 'banana'?
2. Why do you think I want to be a teacher?
3. If I have got ten apples[1] in one hand and seven apples in the other hand, what have I got?
4. If you have got 40p in one pocket and 55p in the other, what have you got?
5. You can't sleep in my class!

a) I know. It's because you talk too much!
b) Big hands.
c) Yes, I do. But I don't know when to stop.
d) In July and August!
e) Somebody else's trousers.

[1][æpl] *Apfel*

1 Spies

a) There are three spies in the room. *Listen and write the names Luigi, Stanislav and Scarlett next to the people.*

b) *Describe what Luigi, Stanislav and Scarlett are doing, and what they are wearing.*

Luigi:

Stanislav:

Scarlett:

2 A report about a friend

Write a short report in your exercise book about someone in your class. Ask him or her questions, and try to find out as much as you can. Here are some ideas:

| where he / she lives | family (brothers or sisters?) | favourite clothes |

| favourite book | hobbies | pets | favourite pop group |

1 Princess Elaine

[1][fi:l] *(sich) fühlen*

Put the numbers in the pictures to show what the people are saying or thinking.

1. "Thank you, Lancelot! You are a good knight."
2. "Guinevere has got one just like it. A clever plan, Dame Brisen!"
3. "What am I doing here? And what are *you* doing here?"
4. "Oh, I feel[1] so tired. I'll just have a little rest."
5. "It will be hard for me, Elaine, but if that's what you want."
6. "Ha ha! Now you are in hot water!"
7. "My baby's name is Galahad. I love him, but I must see his father again or I can never be happy."
8. "Why do you hate me, Morgan le Fay?"
9. "Sir Lancelot, you need a drink. Try this."
10. "Helping princesses is my job, Elaine."
11. "A ring from Guinevere! She loves me! But I must be careful in Camelot. Arthur still loves her."
12. "She's dead. It's too late."
13. "Take this ring, Elaine."
14. "But he loves Guinevere, not me. I must do something!"
15. "Father, if you love me, put me in a boat and send me down the river to Camelot. Please!"
16. "Take this ring to Lancelot. But don't say it's from me."
17. "What a dirty trick, Elaine! Now I hate you and I never want to see you again!"

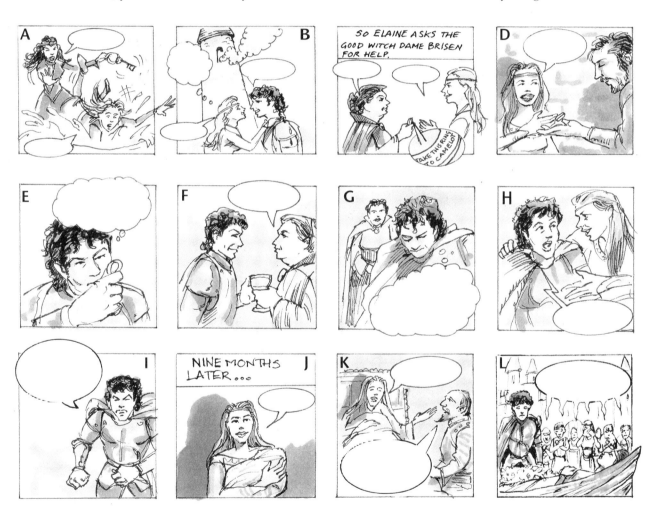

2 About the story

Write the questions and the answers in your exercise book.

Example: 1. Lancelot loved *someone*.   Who did Lancelot love?   He loved Guinevere.

2. Elaine loved *two people*.
3. *Two people* loved Guinevere.
4. *Someone* loved Elaine.
5. *Two people* hated Elaine.
6. *Someone* gave Elaine a ring.
7. Elaine gave the ring to *someone*.
8. Lancelot went *somewhere*.
9. *Someone* died in a boat.

1 Clothes

Put in the words for the clothes.

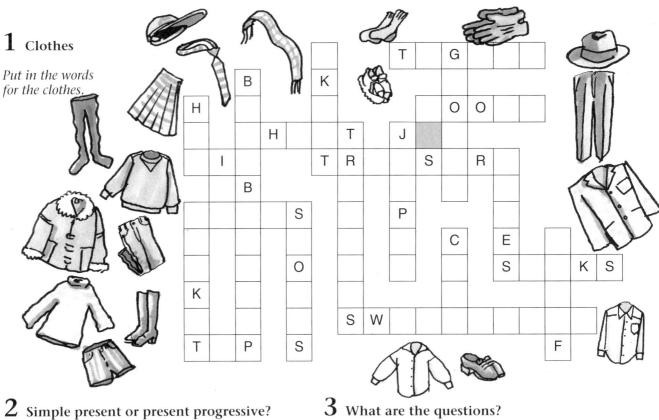

2 Simple present or present progressive?

1. Mr Braden _____ often _____ ties. (not buy)
2. Liam _____ a cup of tea for Mrs Minns now. (make)
3. _____ you _____ to music at the moment? (listen)
4. Liz sometimes _____ her homework at the kitchen table. (do)
5. Mrs Braden usually _____ to work. (drive)
6. Milly _____ in the snow. Look at her! (play)
7. Liz and Liam never _____ the same clothes. (wear)

3 What are the questions?

Write the questions to these answers.

1. _____
   _____
   It means 'to practise', for example for a play or concert.

2. _____
   _____
   S-C-I-S-S-O-R-S.

3. _____
   _____
   Stiefel.

4. _____
   _____
   The sponge is over there, on the desk.

5. _____
   _____
   You buy books in a bookshop, but you borrow them from a library.

4 What happens where?

1. The gym is where
2. The staffroom is where
3. The cafeteria is where
4. The classrooms are where
5. The playground is where
6. The library is where
7. The office is where
8. The assembly hall is where

a) pupils have their lessons.
b) pupils and teachers have lunch.
c) the headteacher works.
d) pupils read or do their homework.
e) pupils and teachers meet in the morning.
f) pupils go in the breaks.
g) pupils do PE.
h) teachers go in the breaks.

60 sixty

UNIT 7

1 By the sea

a) First write down the words for the things in the picture. Then number them.

1. B E A C H
2.
3.
4.
5.
6.
7.
8.
9.
10.
11.
12.

b) Use the words and write a short report about the sea in your exercise book. Say what you can see on the coast and what the people are doing there.

| CHECK-IN | STEP A | STEP B | STEP C | TRACK | CHECK-OUT |

2 One more word

a) *Find one more word with the same sound.*

1. [əʊ] ghost, most, _____
2. [əʊ] no, go, _____
3. [aɪ] fly, die, _____
4. [eɪ] say, day, _____
5. [ɪə] hear, ear, _____
6. [ɪ]   will, still, _____
7. [i:] each, reach, _____
8. [i:] tree, we, _____

b) *Choose three groups and make rhymes¹.*

Example: We can see three birds in the tree.

¹[raɪm] *Reim*

3 Sea words

a) *What are the words?*

| birds by the sea | captains on tankers | people on holiday | slicks of oil | tankers for oil |

seabirds, _____

_____

b) *Use your exercise book and explain these words.*

Example: Volunteers: They help other people or organizations and they don't get any money for it.

volunteers   lighthouse   lifeboat   beachgoers

museum   sailing boat   rubbish

4 Opposites

a) *Find the opposites.*

1. land   _____
2. safe   _____
3. same   _____
4. to live   _____
5. big   _____
6. quiet   _____

7. right   _____
8. inside   _____
9. cheap   _____
10. to buy   _____
11. to produce _____
12. to remember _____

b) *Write sentences with the words in your exercise book. Example:* Plastic is cheap to produce.

| CHECK-IN | **STEP A** | STEP B | STEP C | TRACK | CHECK-OUT |

1 The project group

Complete the sentences with 'going to'.

1. _____ help *Friends of the Earth*.
2. _____ visit the Lighthouse Museum in Penzance.
3. _____ drive the bus.
4. _____ visit the Coastguard in Falmouth.
5. _____ look at the dangerous places.
6. _____ have fish and chips.
7. _____ collect the waste.
8. _____ to the lifeboat teams.

2 What are they going to do?

Make dialogues with these ideas.

1. you / listen to / new CDs / tonight?

   Are you going to listen to your new CDs tonight?

   no / tomorrow

   No, I'm going to listen to them tomorrow.

2. Peter and Jane / sit / behind / Mr Clifford / in the bus?

   Peter and Jane, are you

   no / at the back

   No, we

3. Mr Clifford / phone / Coastguard?

   yes / phone them / after lunch

4. people from the Coastguard / check / all the tankers here?

   yes / all the tankers / in this area

5. you / have fish and chips / in Falmouth?

   no / hot dogs

3 What next?   What are these people going to do?

1. The girl is going to feed the fish.

4. _____

2.  _____

5.  _____

3.  _____

6.  _____

4 What are you going to do next week?

Use your exercise book and write down what you are going to do next week. You can write about your real plans or you can use these ideas:

Mon	Tue	Wed	Thu	Fri	Sat	Sun
help Grandma in the garden + watch tennis on TV.	clean up garage	take modem to computer shop	have piano lesson	play basketball with Mike	go to the cinema with Sue + Ann	have a picnic with Mum + Dad

5 The odd one out

Listen and write down the words. Find the odd one out. Be careful with the spelling of the words.

1. _____   2. _____   3. _____   4. _____

The odd one out in list 1 is _____

The odd one out in list 2 is _____

The odd one out in list 3 is _____

The odd one out in list 4 is _____

1 An article about Britain and the sea

Look at the pictures and put in the words.

GB _____ has more than 2,500 miles of _____ . In many places there are high and dangerous _____ . There are also lovely _____ . But there is a lot of _____ on some of them.

Most of it comes from _____ and _____ . But the rubbish also comes from _____ ; they dump their rubbish _____ . Among the pieces of waste like _____ and _____ are many _____ . _____ help to clean up the beaches. There is an average of 1,500 _____ per kilometre of _____ .

2 Word power   Find another word for:

1. tanker _____
2. to save _____
3. to dispose _____
4. waste _____
5. not clean _____
6. to throw overboard _____
7. every year _____
8. from many countries _____

3 A cinquain

Cinquains[1] are little poems[2] with five lines. 'Cinq' is the French word for 'five'.

There is one word in line one
  (a noun).
There are two words in line two
  (two adjectives to go with the noun).
There are three words in line three
  (three verbs with *-ing*).
There are four words in line four
  (to give more information about the noun).
And there is one word again in line five
  (another noun to go with the noun in line one).

seabirds
big, small
sitting, swimming, flying
live by the sea
friends

[1] ['sɪŋkeɪn] *fünfzeiliges Gedicht* [2] ['pəʊɪm] *Gedicht*

Can you write another cinquain? Think of:

ships – water – ocean – lighthouses – lifeboats – Coastguard – volunteers – holidaymakers

4 On an oil rig

Dave Baxter works on an oil rig[1] in the North Sea.
Listen what he tells you about his job und put in the missing words.

"Well, the money _____ good, but _____ have _____ work for _____ very hard. And _____ have _____ _____ careful too. Our work _____ dangerous. Accidents[2] _____ happen with _____ the machines[3] _____ the rig. _____ always try _____ work well together _____ a team. Sometimes there _____ terrible storms[4]. _____ weather can change _____ quickly out here _____ the North Sea. _____ can't always work _____ the weather _____ bad. Then _____ must wait. That can _____ very boring. _____ usually the time _____ very fast because there's _____ much _____ _____ _____ the rig."

[1][rɪg] *Förderturm* [2]['æksɪdnt] *Unfall* [3][mə'ʃiːn] [4][stɔːm]

5 Homophones

Homophones[1] are two different words with the same sound. *What are they?*

[siː] *sea* / *see*   [raɪt] _____   [hɪə] _____

[nəʊ] _____   [tuː] _____   [ðeə] _____

[baɪ] _____   [nəʊz] _____   [haɪ] _____

[1]['hɒməfəʊn]

6 Adjectives

Find a good adjective to go with these nouns.

1. _____ Beachwatch report
2. _____ beaches
3. _____ bays
4. _____ seabirds
5. _____ plastics
6. _____ volunteers
7. _____ lighthouses
8. _____ captains
9. _____ tankers
10. _____ cliffs
11. _____ oil
12. _____ lifeboats

1 An international dictionary

Freundsprachliches Lexikon

These words are from an international dictionary for children. The children from a Unesco[1] project school have made it.
a) Write in the German and the English words.
b) An idea for a project: You could make an international dictionary too. The German dictionary has got 90 words. Which words would you choose? And which languages[2]?

[1][juːˈneskəʊ] [2][ˈlæŋgwɪdʒ] *Sprache*

	D	RUS	S	NL	J	P	F	KOR	GB	E
👫		ДЕТИ	barn	Kinderen	子供	crianças	enfants	어린이들		Niños
☀️🏖️		КАНИКУЛЫ	skollov	Vakantie	休み	férias	vacances	방학		vacaciones
👬		ДРУЗЬЯ	vänner	Vrienden	友だち	amigos	amis	친구들		amigos
🏙️		ПРАЗДНИК	stad	Stad	市	cidade	ville	도시		ciudad
☀️		СОЛНЦЕ	sol	Zon	太陽	sol	soleil	해		sol
🌞		ЛЕТО	sommar	Zomer	夏	sol	été	여름		verano
🌊		МОРЕ	hav	Zee	海	mar	mer	바다		mar

1 Sounds and spelling

You say [gəʊst] but your write 'ghost'. *What about the spelling of the words on the right?*

You say   You write

[tri:]   _____

[haʊs]   _____

['dʒækɪt] _____

[bəʊt]   _____

[gɜ:l]   _____

[ˌaɪs'kri:m] _____

['laɪthaʊs] _____

[fʊt]   _____

2 Word order

1. dangerous / cliffs / very / high / and / can / rocks / be / wet

_____

2. of / do / just / lie / beaches / and / lots / holidaymakers / nothing / on / the

_____

3. coasts / of / there / on / Britain's / is / a / rubbish / lot

_____

4. along / seabirds / because / thousands / die / of / oil slicks / of / the / coast / the

_____

5. from / over / ships / all / world / the / overboard / rubbish / dump / their

_____

3 Water poem

Translate the poem into German. Use your exercise book.

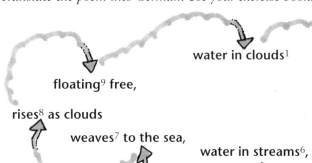

water in clouds[1],
falling as rain[2],
water in gutters[3],
glugging[4] down drains[5],
water in streams[6],
weaves[7] to the sea,
rises[8] as clouds
floating[9] free,

[1][klaʊd] *Wolke*
[2][reɪn] *Regen*
[3]['gʌtə] *Dachrinne*
[4][glʌg] *gluckern*
[5][dreɪn] *Abflussrohr*
[6][stri:m] *Strom*
[7][wi:v] *schlängeln*
[8][raɪz] *aufsteigen*
[9][fləʊt] *schwimmen*

4 What do you think?

Write down what you think.

terrible	boring	dangerous
	interesting	
useful	great	fun	difficult

1. swim — *I think swimming is fun.*
2. play computer games
3. rescue seabirds
4. buy new clothes
5. play an instrument
6. do homework
7. watch football
8. collect rubbish

5 After the warning

After the hurricane warning people are usually worried. Mr Richards is talking to his neighbour about the latest news. *Complete their dialogue.*

Will the storm hit the coast? What do you think?

Well, I think, yes, _____ .

I'm sure _____ turn north.

You never know. Perhaps it _____, perhaps it _____ .

Let's hope the damage _____ too bad.

Yes. Maybe it _____ just break some windows.

When it turns west _____ cross Florida.

Well, I think _____ east and churn into the Atlantic.

_____ emergency services?

Yes, _____ _____ at all the evacuation points.

OK. _____ have to wait and see.

| CHECK-IN | STEP A | STEP B | STEP C | TRACK | **CHECK-OUT** |

1 The seasons

These signs are very old. You can find them on old stones. They stand for the four seasons.
Use them for a word bank and write nouns that go with the seasons.

 SPRING

 SUMMER

 AUTUMN

 WINTER

flowers   *ice cream*   *windy*   *snow*

2 The odd one out

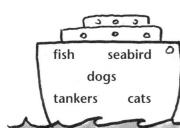 fish, seabird, dogs, tankers, cats

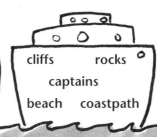 cliffs, rocks, captains, beach, coastpath

 children, boys, holidaymakers, teachers, women

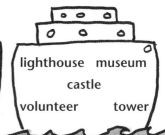 lighthouse, museum, castle, volunteer, tower

The odd one out is:

1. _____ 2. _____ 3. _____ 4. _____

3 The seaside alphabet

A _____
B _____
C _____
D _____
E _____
F _____
G _____
H _____
I _____
J _____
K *kids*
L _____
M _____
N _____
O _____
P _____
Q *quick*
R _____
S _____
T _____
U *uniform*
V _____
W _____
X *xxx*
Y *young*
Z _____

70 seventy

UNIT 8

1 What would they like to do?

Look at what these kids are thinking. Can you say what activities they would like to take part in? Use your exercise book. And maybe you can also say in what ways they would like to take part, what things they would like to do.

paint	sing	play
go to	go on	sail
act	make	sell
write	work	

Mike Joan Ellen Liam

Pat Pete Liz

2 More activities

Look at these new notices. Would you like to take part in these activities? Say why, or why not.

I'd like to ... / wouldn't like to ...   I like / don't like / hate ...
... is interesting / fun / boring / great / ...

Tennis tournament[1]
Juniors:
First round[2] 28th April
Finals[3] 12th May
Seniors:
First round 5th May
Finals 19th May

Learn the Cornish language[4]**!**
Lessons with Ms Trelawne every Tuesday this term,
4 and 5 pm

Video show
Last year's sailing trip to the Isles of Scilly
Monday 15th May, 4 pm
Room 107

[1] ['tʊənəmənt] *Turnier* [2] [raʊnd] *hier: Runde* [3] ['faɪnl] *Endspiel* [4] ['kɔːnɪʃ 'læŋgwɪdʒ] *alte keltische Sprache Cornwalls*

| CHECK-IN | **STEP A** | STEP B | STEP C | TRACK | CHECK-OUT |

1 Regular and irregular verbs

Find the past participles of these verbs and put them in the right list.

happen	clean	see	ask	be
change	put	damage	leave	collect
phone	think	practise	do	close
go	make	open	find	get

regular	irregular
to happen — happened	*to see —*

2 The accident

a) *Put in the past participles to make the present perfect.*

– Look, there's water on the floor! I think someone has _____ the tap¹ on². — leave

– No, it's that water tank over there, there's something wrong with it. Look, it has _____ quite full, and the water is running over the top! — get

– Oh dear, you're right. And it has _____ everything wet³ in that corner. These boxes, for example. Do you know what's in them? — make

– No idea. But I think I've _____ Maggie and Andrew with them. Must be something to do with the drama club. Let's take a look. — see

– But it's not easy to open them. They've _____ them well, and _____ sticky tape³ on top! — close / put

– Here, I've _____ a knife, use that. — find

– It's OK, I've already _____ this one. Yuk, what a mess⁴! — open

b) *Now put in the full present perfect forms.*

– Looks like costumes of some kind. But it can't be the King Arthur costumes, can it? I _____ them before, and they are nice colours: green, yellow, red, etc. with gold bits on them. These are all grey and brown! — see

– Oh-oh, they're the King Arthur costumes all right. Look at this: the water _____ it, and it isn't gold any more, but you can see it's a crown! — damage

– You're right. And the clothes _____ grey because they _____ in the water so long. — go / be

– So we must find Andrew and Maggie and tell them about this. They don't know it yet, but I think this _____ all their plans ... — change

¹[tæp] *Wasserhahn* ²*hier: eingeschaltet, an* ³[teɪp] *Klebeband* ⁴[mes] *Durcheinander, Schlamassel*

3 My favourites

a) *What is your favourite book*?
How many times have you read it?
And why do you like it so much?
And what about films*, CDs*, etc.?
Write three sentences about each.*

book	read	(only) once[1]	great
film	see	twice	very ...
CD / record	listen to / hear	three ...	exciting
TV programme	watch / see	twenty times	interesting
		lots of	funny

**The names can be in English or German or ...*

Example: My favourite ... is ... . I've (already) ... it ... times. I think it's ... .

b) *And perhaps you've got some other favourites?
Write about them in your exercise book.*

a poem	–	read
a story	–	read / listen to
a song	–	hear / listen to / sing
food	–	eat / cook[2] / make
a T-shirt	–	wear
...		

[1][wʌns] *einmal* [2][kʊk] *kochen*

4 Have they done it yet?

[1]dye [daɪ] *(Haar) Färbemittel*

a) *Look at the pictures and ask the questions.*

John and Sue / paint ...   Ellen / write ...   Steve / pack ...

_____?   _____?   _____?

Yes, they have.   *No, she hasn't.*   *No, he hasn't.*

5 Cartoons

Which words go with which cartoons? Write them in.

YOU'VE WASTED¹ YOUR MONEY!

"Mummy, Mummy! Daddy's batteries² have run out³!"

"Melvin? He's gone to his weekend box in the country."

¹[weɪst] *verschwenden*
²['bætri]
³*hier: leer werden*

_____

*
_____

_____

6 Have you ever …?

Here are some more ideas for 'Have you ever …?' questions.

see a ghost   meet a famous person
run a marathon   see a UFO¹
fall into water   have an adventure

a) *Write out the questions in your exercise book – and answer them.*

b) *Now pick out one of the questions where you answered with 'Yes, I have.' (It can be one from your English book, page 127.) Write out this question and answer here, and then tell your story. Remember, now you want to talk about an exact time or place, and say what you did or saw, what happened to you, who you met. So use the past tense for your story!*

You can start: It happened …
I saw one … yesterday / last night / week / October / …
It was in …

Have you ever
Yes, I have.

_____
_____
_____
_____

If you have more than one story, write the others in your exercise book.

¹[juːˈefˈəʊ]

1 Enid Blyton

When you are reading something new in English, you don't need to know every word. You can always guess a lot.

a) *Try this with the text on the back of the Enid Blyton book. (Just a little help: A 'centenary' [sen'ti:nəri] is someone's 100th birthday.)*

b) *Now show what you have understood. What new words in the text must mean the same as:*

big _____

find _____

sending signals _____

And which new words must mean:

unterirdisch _____

erwischen _____

entzückt _____

Generationen _____

Sammler _____

Ausgabe, Edition _____

gedenken _____

Geburt _____

> **Five Go To Smuggler's Top**
>
> # THE FAMOUS FIVE
>
> Are there still smugglers at Smuggler's Top? The Famous Five go to stay at the large, old house and discover hiding places and underground tunnels! Then they catch people signalling out to sea – who can they be?
>
> *Enid Blyton's books have delighted generations of children. These special collectors' editions commemorate the centenary of her birth.*
>
> ISBN 0-340-68109-8
> UK £3.99

c) *Now say why it is easy to guess the new words. Put the right number next to the word.*

I can guess it
I know it

1. from what the other words in the sentence mean,
2. because I've learned an English word like the new one,
3. because it's like a German word.

2 Smugglers in Cornwall

Cornwall has always been a great place for smugglers. *Try to explain why. Write a sentence about each of these things and facts, and why smugglers like them.*

(the sea) _____
_____

(caves) _____
_____

(not many towns) _____
_____

1 Those funny sounds again!

Put these words in the right 'sound boxes'. Be careful: some words can go in more than one box! Mark the letter(s) with the sound.

Penzance   King Arthur
   sand   together
concert   than   thin
   Falmouth   weather
father   cousin   to use
   to bother   throws
summer   nothing
   Robinson   Burns

[s]	[z]

[θ]	[ð]

2 What has just happened?

Look at the cartoons. They haven't got any real words, but you can see what's funny about them, can't you? Write out what has just happened. Some words and phrases to help you:

to learn a language   animals
   ['læŋgwɪdʒ] (*Sprache*)   to go down
to cut (*past part.*: cut)   ship
   [kʌt] (*schneiden*)   hair

3 The all-purpose[1] children's poem   by Roger McGough [məˈgʌf]

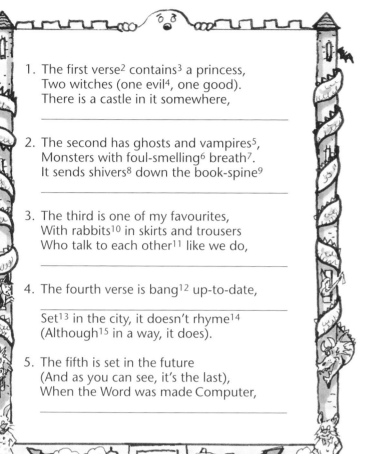

1. The first verse[2] contains[3] a princess,
   Two witches (one evil[4], one good).
   There is a castle in it somewhere,
   _____

2. The second has ghosts and vampires[5],
   Monsters with foul-smelling[6] breath[7].
   It sends shivers[8] down the book-spine[9]
   _____

3. The third is one of my favourites,
   With rabbits[10] in skirts and trousers
   Who talk to each other[11] like we do,
   _____

4. The fourth verse is bang[12] up-to-date,
   _____
   Set[13] in the city, it doesn't rhyme[14]
   (Although[15] in a way, it does).

5. The fifth is set in the future
   (And as you can see, it's the last),
   When the Word was made Computer,
   _____

[1][ˌɔːlˈpɜːpəs] *Allzweck-* [2][vɜːs] *Strophe*
[3][kənˈteɪn] *enthalten* [4][ˈiːvl] *böse* [5][ˈvæmpaɪə]
[6][ˌfaʊlˈsmelɪŋ] *übel riechend* [7][breθ] *Atem*
[8][ˈʃɪvə] *Schaudern* [9][ˈbʊkspaɪn] *Buchrücken*
[10][ˈræbɪt] *Kaninchen* [11][ˌiːtʃˈʌðə] *miteinander*
[12][bæŋ] *hier: ganz, absolut* [13][set] *es spielt*
[14][raɪm] *reimen* [15][ɔːlˈðəʊ] *obwohl* [16][niːt] *nett,
hübsch* [17][ˈtæŋgld] *verflochten* [18]*hier: alles ist
erlaubt* [19][ˈskeə] *erschrecken* [20][deθ] *(zu) Tode*

a) *Some lines have fallen out of the poem! Put them back in the right places.*

And books are a thing of the past.

And live in neat[16] little houses.

And a dark and tangled[17] wood.

And in it, anything goes[18].

And scares[19] everybody to death[20].

b) *Now complete this dialogue with the right words.*

some	any	no	every
-body	-thing	-where	

After this poem maybe you don't need _____ other one – it's got _____ !

Well, not really. It hasn't got _____ pirates.
And there's _____ about the sea.

No. But it's got _____ witches, and ghosts, and monsters!
_____ verse has got _____ different!

But _____ animals. I like poems about animals.

Oh, yes, it has. It's got _____ rabbits!

Rabbits? I don't see _____ rabbits _____ !

Oh, dear, can't you find _____ yourself? It's … er …

Hm, I'm sure there are _____ rabbits there _____ ! Yes, there, in the third verse!

OK, but _____ can say they're real. Real animals don't wear _____ clothes – _____ knows that!

Oh, you can't be happy with _____ .
Go write your own all-purpose poem!

1 Southernmost crossword

Across

2. You can see two different ... from Islamorada!
4. See 12. across.
6. It's too ... for most (7. down) in the summer.
10. Key West is a ... place, says B. J.
11. See 12. across.
12., 4., + 11. The sea of the west coast.
13. See 11. down.
14. You must be ... to go there in the summer.
15. Many (30. down) still live on a ... .
18. Maybe you ... go in the summer – hotels are cheap.
19. See 16. down.
20. Osceola was a ... hero.
22. + 3. down. You ... ... two seas from Islamorada.
23. B. J., are you on the ocean or the gulf ... of the island?
25. Terrible storms from the sea.
26. A city in the middle of the state.
28. You can also ... on two seas from Islamorada.
31. When doesn't the sun shine? Only when it's ... .
33. This is a very ... state.
34. Let's go to (26. across) – ... World is there!
37. Sailing is a great water ... .
38. + 17. down. A place on the east coast (think of NASA).

Down

1. ... dear! It's much too (6. across) for me.
2. Lots of people come here for the ... .
3. See 22. across.
5. The name of the state.
7. Most ... come in the winter.
8. The (32. down) are ... the south coast.
9. Most (25. across) ... the east coast first.
11. + 13. across. A big city on the east coast.
16. + 19. across. The sea off the east coast.
17. See 38. across.
19. The ... Highway goes all the way to Key West.
21. You can see lots of interesting animals and birds in the ... .
24. This ... a great place for sailing and swimming.
27. Does B. J like it hot ... cold?
29. In this month it's really very (6. across).
30. The (20. across) are a group of ... .
32. The islands of the south coast.
35. No, B. J., there are ... hurricanes in Cornwall.
36. The summer is ... hot for most (7. down).

78 *seventy-eight*

2 Before and after Hurricane Andrew

B. J.'s elder sister keeps a diary. *Read what she wrote on four different days, and put in the verb in the right form.* a) *Present simple, present progressive or present perfect?*

August 23, 1992
Everybody _____ about the hurricane. It _____ here yet, but every hour the weatherman _____ on TV and _____ us where it _____. Just now it _____ near the Bahamas, and _____ nearer all the time. They _____ it will hit the south coast in the night, but _____ sure exactly where. Mum _____ we must be ready: hurricane _____ the Keys many times before. I _____ it's exciting — I _____ a real hurricane yet!

talk — not get
come — tell
be — be
come — think
not be
say — hit
think — never see

August 24, 1992
It _____ here! The winds _____ stronger all the time. The palm¹ trees _____ the ground²! Of course, we _____ all the doors and windows and _____ up shutters³. Dad _____ in his boat. It _____ now late at night but I _____ to go to bed — it _____ too exciting! — Wow! Something _____ upstairs — I _____ a window _____, or something. And the lights _____ out ...

be — get
touch — close
put — bring
be — not want
be — happen
think — break
go

b) *Use any of those tenses — or the past tense.*

August 25, 1992
That _____ awful last night! But we _____ OK. We still _____ a roof over our heads. We _____ our electricity back yet, so no TV. But Mum's transistor radio⁴ still _____, and we _____ the news. At about two in the morning, Andrew _____ the Florida coast about a hundred miles north of here. One of their reporters _____ in Homestead⁵ (just south of Miami) in the middle of the storm, and she _____ what it was like there in the night. And what it _____ like there now: Andrew _____ all of the houses there, she _____. Most of the people _____ nowhere to stay! Oh dear! What about Aunt Zoe⁶ and family on the reservation? That _____ very near Homestead! — We _____ to get Zoe on the phone, but the phone _____. Of course!

be — be
have — not get
work
just hear — hit
be
describe
be
damage — say
have
be — try
not work

August 26, 1992
Zoe and the kids _____ here late last night, and _____ us their story. About three o'clock the night before last, Andrew _____ the roof off their house, and they all _____ wet! They _____ OK now, but their house _____ a mess, all their things _____ damaged. They _____ to clean up yet, because they can't get anything anywhere. Andrew _____ all the shops there too!

come — tell
take
get — be
be — get
not start
damage

¹[pɑːm] *Palme* ²[graʊnd] *Boden* ³[ˈʃʌtə] *Fensterladen* ⁴[ˈreɪdɪəʊ] ⁵[ˈhəʊmsted] ⁶[ˈzəʊi]

1 What has changed for the Braden family?

A lot of things have changed for the Braden family since they left London. *Write out one or two things for each of the Bradens. Use your exercise book.*

Example: Max and Milly have stopped fighting.
(Well, most of the time!)

Here are some ideas for the others. (You must know or guess who has done what, of course!)

"There's a little animal in the kitchen and it's eating cheese. I understand it's your department."

[1][dʒɔɪn] *Mitglied werden (bei)*

> make a lot of new friends at school   open a new workshop for old chairs and tables
> learn to sail   take Milly for lots of country walks   start an astronomy club
> start a new job with a Cornwall newspaper   join[1] the computer club
> write a play   learn some Cornish (because her family is from there!)

2 Cornwall tourists

Put in the right words.

some	any	no	every
-thing	-body	-where	

1 – Have you seen my camera[1] _____ ? I've been careful to put it _____ safe, but now

I can't find it! I've looked _____ , and I have _____ idea where it can be.

2 – Have you _____ idea where we are?

– I think we're ... er ... here, not far from Penzance.

– But then there must be a castle _____ near.

I can't see _____ castle, can you?

– There's _____ over there ... No, it's just a house.

– So we're in the middle of _____ , and can't find

our way back.

– We can ask _____ .

– But there isn't _____ around to ask!

3 – There's that nice café. _____ says it's very good. Let's try it.

– OK, but only if they've got _____ solid[2], like chips. I'm hungry!

Hm ... No, they haven't got _____ for me. Only sandwiches[3] ...

– Oh, don't be silly! _____ nice sandwiches are just right for now.

[1]['kæmrə] *Fotoapparat* [2]['sɒlɪd] *fest, solide* [3]['sænwɪdʒ]

UNIT 9

1 Braintrainer

A group of detectives from INTERPOL are on a flight to London. One of them is not really a detective, but a bank robber. *Find out who is sitting where, and write which country the bank robber is from.*

Pilot	A	C	E	G	I
Co-pilot	B	D	F	H	J

The detective behind the pilot is Irish.
The detective from England is sitting behind the Indian detective.
The detective from Scotland is behind the French detective.
The detective next to the Italian speaks English, but isn't American.
The bank robber is drinking a glass of wine.
The Welsh detective is sitting in the second row.
The Turkish detective is on the right of the detective from Wales.
The Indian detective is sitting on the left of the Scottish detective.
The bank robber is sitting two rows from the German on the same side.
The detectives in the front row speak the same language.
The Italian detective is in the last row.
The German detective is in the third row.
Only the detectives in the first and fourth rows are drinking.

The bank robber is from _____ .

2 May I or must I?

Use 'can' / 'can't', 'may' / 'may not', 'must' / 'mustn't', or 'needn't'.

1. You _____ carry a tent with you.
2. With a campervan you _____ be more independent.
3. It _____ be worse than last year.
4. You _____ wear these clothes at school.
5. You _____ swim in the canal.
6. _____ I go to London by train?
7. You _____ get away from it all for the weekend.
8. You _____ take a lot of things with you.

3 Adjective-noun pairs

Find seven more adjective-noun pairs and write sentences to show you know what they mean. Use your exercise book.

bouncy	swimming pool	guide	countryside	walking
music	useful	gear	necessary	heated	cheap
live	experience	castle	wild	accommodation

Example: This guide to cycling tours in Ireland is very useful. It has got everything you need to know.

| CHECK-IN | STEP A | STEP B | STEP C | TRACK | CHECK-OUT |

4 From the Youth Hostel Handbook

a) *Read this text from the International Youth Hostel Handbook. Mark the key words and important information.*

Your Youth Hostel Travel Guide

What are youth hostels?

- Youth hostels provide low-cost accommodation to young people on their travels.
- They are very different from country to country and even within a country. Some hostels are in old houses, castles or modern buildings, but you will also find hostels which provide the most basic accommodation.
- They provide separate sleeping accommodation and washing and toilet facilities for men and for women. Accommodation is usually in dormitories (generally bunk beds), sometimes with as few as four beds, sometimes with as many as 20.
- Usually there is a common room, where hostellers can meet on an informal basis.
- There may be facilities for guests to cook their own meals.
- Hostels are run by 'hostel managers', 'wardens' or 'houseparents', who in many cases provide the meals. In large hostels there is often a cafeteria.
- In smaller hostels guests are often asked to help with work around the hostel (cleaning, sweeping out their room, etc).
- Youth hostels do not usually offer hotel standards of comfort and service, but many provide quality accommodation and facilities.

Hostel information

- Smoking is not allowed in the dormitories (as the fire risk would be too great). The consumption of alcohol is also forbidden.
- You cannot normally stay more than three consecutive nights at the same youth hostel. Rules are different for ski-parties, school groups and during the off-season.

b) *Choose the right answer or complete the sentences.*

1. If the verb 'to travel' means *reisen*, the noun 'travel' means _____ .
2. 'Provide' means a) give, b) take?
3. If accommodation is low-cost, it is very c _ _ _ p.
4. Are the prices for accommodation in the off-season a) high, or b) low?
5. If youth hostels vary greatly, they can be very d _ f f _ _ _ _ t .
6. Is basic accommodation a) very simple, or b) very comfortable?
7. If things are separate, they are not t _ _ _ t _ _ _ r.
8. A dormitory is a big room where people a) sleep, b) eat, c) do sports.
9. The word 'generally' means a) usually, b) never, c) always.
10. 'As few as' is the opposite of 'as _ _ _ _ as'.
11. 'Large' means the same as b _ g, and the opposite of s _ _ _ l.
12. 'Consecutive' means a) one after the other, b) with breaks between.
13. Economical meals are not too e _ _ _ _ _ _ v _ .
14. If something is forbidden, a) you should do it, b) you should not do it.

c) *Imagine you work in a big youth hostel. What do you tell people who ask you these questions? Write your answers in your exercise book.*

1. "Is it possible to stay for a whole week? I'm not travelling in a group." (It is July.)
2. "We're having a party in the dormitory. Come and drink some wine with us!"
3. "Is there somewhere where we can just sit, play cards and talk?"
5. "Do all youth hostels have a cafeteria? And who cooks the meals?"
4. "I don't like youth hostel food. Can I make my own meals?"
5. "Do men and women use the same bathrooms?"
6. "Why can't we smoke in the dormitories?"

1 Around the British Isles

a) *Write the places on the map.*

The Republic of Ireland
Northern Ireland
Wales
Scotland
England
East Anglia
London
Belfast
Dublin
Cardiff
Edinburgh
Brighton

b) *Four people in a pub are talking about the British Isles. Listen and write the descriptions on the map in the right places.*

wettest
driest
flattest
warmest
coldest
sunniest
most expensive
highest mountain[1]
lowest population[2]

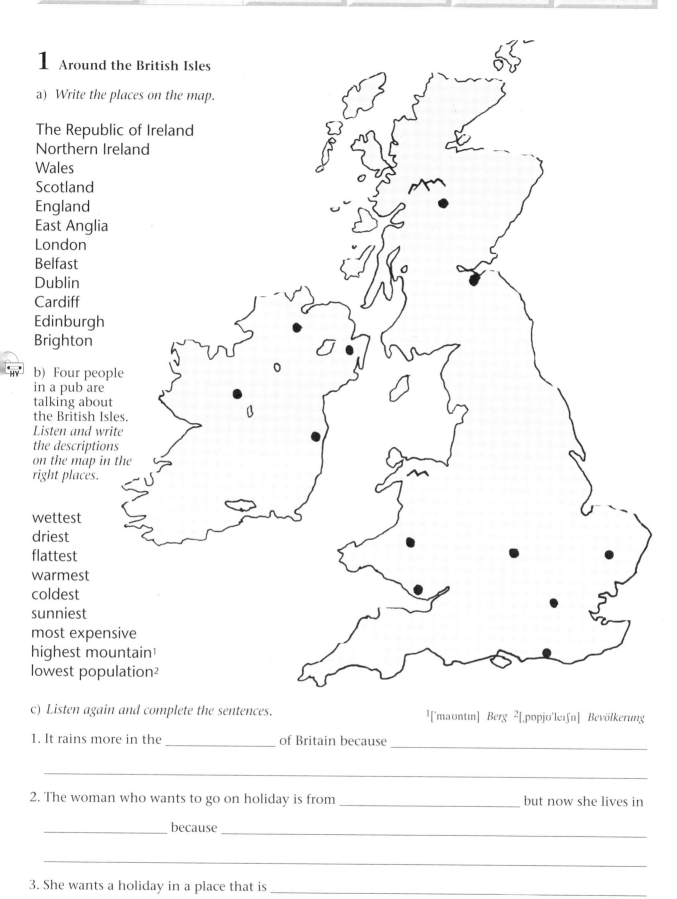

[1] ['maʊntɪn] *Berg* [2] [ˌpɒpjʊ'leɪʃn] *Bevölkerung*

c) *Listen again and complete the sentences.*

1. It rains more in the _____ of Britain because _____
   _____

2. The woman who wants to go on holiday is from _____ but now she lives in
   _____ because _____
   _____

3. She wants a holiday in a place that is _____
   and which has got _____ so that she can _____

d) *Suggest where the woman should go on holiday, and explain why. (The place can be outside the British Isles.)*

_____
_____

2 Comparatives and superlatives

a) *Write the comparative and superlative forms of these adjectives.*

1. long, _____
2. easy, _____
3. good, _____
4. traditional, _____

5. safe, _____
6. bad, _____
7. big, _____
8. beautiful, _____

b) *Put in a comparative or superlative form of an adjective. Then answer the question.*

1. Which is the ___worst___ day of the week for you? _____
2. Which do you think are _____ – dogs or cats? _____
3. Which is the _____ day of the year? _____
4. Which is _____ – a dictionary or a comic? _____
5. Which is _____ – The Republic of Ireland or Northern Ireland? _____

3 Teapots

a) *Write about the teapots. Use the comparative forms of the adjectives.*

| Teapot A | Teapot B | Teapot C | Teapot D |

interesting   heavy   expensive   useful   big
funny   old   small   big   cheap

1. *A is funnier than C, but it isn't as useful.*
2. *C* _____ *D,* _____
3. *A* _____ *B,* _____
4. *B* _____ *D,* _____
5. *B* _____ *C,* _____

b) *Choose four adjectives from a) and put in the superlative forms.*

1. Teapot A is the _____ .
2. Teapot B is the _____ .
3. Teapot C is the _____ .
4. Teapot D is the _____ .

1 A hotel in Deal

The writer Paul Theroux is travelling around the coast of Britain, by train and on foot.

At no point in three months of travel did I have a reservation in advance, at a hotel or a guest-house. I wanted to come and go as I pleased and not to be held to specific places and dates. I thought: If I can't get a room I'll move on to another place and look – but that was never necessary. I never found a hotel that was full, though I found many that were completely empty. I was never sent away.

Some of the hotel owners or guest-house proprietors were embarrassed by their empty rooms. Some said it was early in the season. "We'll be packed in June", they said in May. But in June they said, "Things are quiet now, but it'll be a madhouse in July when the school holidays start." In July they said, "In August we're always fully booked." But they were nearly always empty. Some of the owners said that people had stopped travelling in Britain – they went to Spain when they went at all. Some said, "It's this recession. It's a world-wide problem." Some people said, "We're not a rich country any more. We're poor." It was these people who always overcharged me.

My method of finding a place to stay was to walk up and down the streets and to look for a clean or well-shaped building that had a view of the sea. I did not try the new hotel (too expensive) or the place in which I heard music playing (too noisy) or the damp place in a back lane (stinks and hard beds).

The tall hotel I found in Deal after walking around for twenty minutes looked all right – it had lovely windows; but as soon as I went in I saw it was no good. It smelled of bacon and beer, and it was run by a fat dirty woman named Mrs Sneath, who smoked in my face.

"Cheapest single room I have is ten pounds," Mrs Sneath said. "That's bed and full breakfast."

"Your sign says the room starts at seven pounds."

"I don't have any left, do I," she said.

"I'll take a ten pound room."

"With tax that's eleven pounds fifty," she said as she wrote out the bill, "in advance."

From *The Kingdom by the Sea* by Paul Theroux

a) *True or false?*

1. Paul Theroux didn't make reservations when he travelled.
2. It was hard to find accommodation because most places were full.
3. Only poor people from Spain travel in Britain.
4. He wanted a place where he could see the sea.
5. If he could hear loud music, he didn't ask for a room.
6. He found somewhere to stay in Deal after half an hour.
7. Mrs Sneath was a thin woman, and not very clean.
8. Paul Theroux paid more than the price on the sign.

b) *Correct the four false sentences.*

1. _____
2. _____
3. _____
4. _____

2 Find out ...

Answer the questions about the text.

1. How long did Paul Theroux travel around Britain. During which months?

2. What did he notice about all the hotels and guest houses?

3. What things does he not like about some of them?

4. Who is Mrs Sneath? Do you think Paul likes her? Why, or why not?

3 Vocabulary

How many pairs of opposites can you find in the text? Mark them in the text, and then list them below.

up — down, empty —

4 Creative writing

a) You are Mrs Sneath. You did not have many guests last summer so you are going to put an advertisement in the newspapers. Write the text for the advertisement. Make your hotel – and Deal – sound as attractive as possible.

b) You are an inspector from the 'Good Hotel Guide'. You have visited Mrs Sneath's hotel, and it was a shock. Write a report.

1 Things in common

Tessa has a lot in common with Nathan, but not with Clark. *Write what she says.*

1. *Nathan:* I love ghost stories.   *Tessa:* So do I!
2. *Nathan:* I can stand on my head.   *Tessa:* _____
3. *Nathan:* I don't like Mondays.   *Tessa:* _____
4. *Nathan:* I've got the King Kong video.   *Tessa:* _____
5. *Clark:* I always eat big breakfasts.   *Tessa:* Do you? I don't.
6. *Clark:* I've never read Enid Blyton.   *Tessa:* _____
7. *Clark:* I'm a Madonna fan.   *Tessa:* _____
8. *Clark:* I'd like a really fast motorbike.   *Tessa:* _____

2 Choosing between phrases

Find the pairs with the same meaning. Then underline the more formal phrase.

1. Dear Ms Clifton, ...
2. Thanks a lot for ...
3. Write back soon!
4. Love, ...
5. I would be grateful for some information on ...

a) I look forward to hearing from you.
b) Yours faithfully, ...
c) I'd like some info on ...
d) Thank you very much for ...
e) Hi there, Tessa!

3 Words for letters – letters for words   *Complete the gaps.*

Dear Sir or M _ _ _ _ ,

My family w _ _ _ _ like to go on a walking holiday in the British Isles next summer. Please w _ _ _ _ y _ _ s _ _ _ us some brochures with i _ _ _ _ _ _ _ _ _ _ _ _ about travel and a _ _ _ _ _ _ _ _ _ _ _ _ _ _ .

We w _ _ _ _ also be g _ _ _ _ _ _ _ _ _ f _ _ tips on interesting places to visit, and some maps and guides w _ _ _ be u _ _ _ _ _ too. P _ _ _ _ _ _ also l _ _ us k _ _ _ if we can take our dog with us. We l _ _ _ f _ _ _ _ _ _ _ to h _ _ _ _ _ from you soon.

Yours f _ _ _ _ _ _ _ _ _ _ _ ,

Shirley Brown

1 A postcard to America

a) Steve, the American boy from Chicago, is youth hostelling in England with his school class. *Listen and tick the boxes.*

b) *Write the text of Steve's postcard. (If you like, you can add more details.)*

_____

_____

_____

_____

_____

¹purpose [ˈpɜːpəs] *Zweck* ²appropriate [əˈprɒpɪət] *zutreffend* ³varied [ˈværɪd] *unterschiedlich* ⁴rotten [ˈrɒtn] *miserabel*
⁵journey [ˈdʒɜːni] *Reise* ⁶regards [rɪˈɡɑːdz] *Grüße* ⁷government department [ˈɡʌvnmənt dɪˈpɑːtmənt] *Regierungsabteilung*

1 Question tags

Put in the question tags.

1. The weather is dreadful,
2. There are 30 days in September,
3. You haven't forgotten the key,
4. He'll be at the party,
5. Steve doesn't come from Florida,
6. The Wilsons liked the campervan,
7. Tarkan can speak Turkish,
8. You weren't at the disco last night,

a) _____
b) _____
c) _____
d) _____
e) _____
f) _____
g) _____
h) _____

2 Adjectives to adverbs

1. Maike is a slow swimmer. *Maike swims* _____
2. Jimmy is a good tennis player. _____
3. Geri isn't a bad singer. _____
4. Mr Clifton is a careful driver. _____
5. Liz is a regular letter writer. _____
6. Sandra isn't a fast runner. _____
7. Mr Modi is a hard worker. _____

3 Adjective or adverb?

Complete the sentences. Change the adjectives to adverbs where necessary.

| slow | easy | hungry | fast | frequent | good | bad |

1. Whitewater rafting is dangerous! I've had some _____ experiences!
2. Milly looked _____ at the bacon.
3. Mr Modi _____ works late.
4. I can speak French, but I'm not so _____ at writing it.
5. You're driving too _____ ! What's the hurry?
6. It's not difficult at all. You can do it _____ .
7. It's a _____ train. It only goes 30 miles an hour.

1 The big *Swift* quiz

1. The third month of the year is _____ . August is the _____ .

2. Monday, _____ , Wednesday, _____ .

3. One watch, two _____ . One knife, two _____ .

4. See, _____ , seen. Go, _____ , gone.

5. The British and American flags are _____ , _____ and blue.

6. The comparative and superlative of 'easy': _____ , _____

7. What is the time? *Write it out in words.*

    _____

    _____

8. *Underline the correct form. Cross out the wrong form.*

   a) Tarkan (usually goes / is usually going) to school on his bike.

   b) What (do you do / are you doing) at the moment?

9. *Name the tenses:*

   a) Max likes Milly. _____

   b) I am doing a quiz. _____

   c) The Bradens have moved to Cornwall. _____

10. *Name three school subjects.*

    a) _____   b) _____   c) _____

11. When do you say 'some' and when do you say 'any'? *(You can write the answer in German.)*
    _____

12. *Write the opposites:*

    a) to laugh _____   b) to break _____   c) to find _____

13. *Colour the nouns in red, the pronouns in orange, the verbs in blue, the prepositions in green, the adjectives in yellow, and the adverbs in brown.*

    a) I hate horrible smells!   c) You speak English well!

    b) Your glasses are under the table. d) Break the eggs carefully onto the plate.

14. *What is the difference between the two sentences? (You can explain in German.)*

    a) I'm going to go to the cinema.   b) I'm going to the cinema.
    _____

15. *Add three words to each list.*

    a) animals: cat, _____

b) musical instruments: piano, _____

c) seasons: spring, _____

d) food: sausages, _____

e) jobs: reporter, _____

16. *Write the word with 'is' or 'are':*

   a) My _____ too short. c) This _____ dirty.

   b) Where ____ my _____ ? d) _____ my _____ in your room?

17. I – my, you – _____, he – _____, she – _____, we – _____, they – _____

18. *Put in the countries:*

   a) Cardiff is in _____ .   e) Liverpool is in _____ .

   b) Belfast is in _____ .   f) Paris is in _____ .

   c) Glasgow is in _____ .   g) Stuttgart is in _____ .

   d) Ankara is in _____ .   h) Chicago is in _____ .

19. *Sort the phrases into groups.*

   You're wrong. – Yes, I think so, too. – That's rubbish! – Why don't we …? – That's right.

   Let's … – How about …? – I don't agree. – Very true! – We could …

Agreeing	Disagreeing	Making suggestions

20. *Match the words that rhyme.*

   blue – start – high – please – row – sight – why – go – heart

   heard – bird – shoe – these – white

   _____

   _____

21. *Write the nouns.*

   a) safe _____   b) dangerous _____   c) to describe _____

22. *Put in the right forms of the verbs.*

   a) "_____ you _____ your English homework at the moment?" (do)

   b) "Yes, I _____ irregular verbs." (practise)

   c) "_____ n't you _____ them yet?" (learn)

   d) "Well, we only _____ English last year!" (start)

   e) "Oh, I see. So pupils usually _____ English later at your school?" (start)

   f) "That's right. We _____ just _____ the first book." (finish)

GRAMMAR

Das Präsens (einfache Form) – The simple present

Das *simple present* brauchst du, um über gewohnheitsmäßige, d.h. immer wiederkehrende Handlungen zu sprechen. Signalwörter: *always, sometimes, often, usually, never*.

Aussage	Frage	Verneinung
I eat … .	Do I eat …?	No, I don't.
You eat … .	Do you eat …?	No, you don't.
He eat**s** … .	**Does** he eat …?	No, he doesn't.
She eat**s** … .	**Does** she eat …?	No, she doesn't.
It eat**s** … .	**Does** it eat …?	No, it doesn't.
We eat … .	Do we eat …?	No, we don't.
You eat … .	Do you eat …?	No, you don't.
They eat … .	Do they eat …?	No, they don't.

He, she, it – das ‚s' muss mit!

Die Verlaufsform – The present progressive

Das *present progressive* brauchst du, wenn du sagen willst, was jemand gerade (nicht) macht.
Bildung: *am / is / are + verb + -ing*. Signalwörter: *now, at the moment, just* usw.

Aussage			Frage		Verneinung		
I'm	(I am)	read**ing** … .	(What)	am I do**ing**?	I'm not	(I am not)	read**ing** … .
You're	(you are)	go**ing** … .	(When)	are you go**ing**?	You aren't	(you are not)	go**ing** … .
He's	(he is)	meet**ing** … .	(Who)	is he meet**ing**?	He isn't	(he is not)	meet**ing** … .
She's	(she is)	sitt**ing** … .	(Where)	is she sitt**ing**?	She isn't	(she is not)	sitt**ing** … .
It's	(it is)	ly**ing** … .	(Where)	is it ly**ing**?	It isn't	(it is not)	ly**ing** … .
We're	(we are)	com**ing** … .	(What)	are we do**ing**?	We aren't	(we are not)	com**ing** … .
You're	(you are)	look**ing** … .	(Why)	are you look**ing**?	You aren't	(you are not)	look**ing** … .
They're	(they are)	tak**ing** … .	(What)	are they tak**ing**?	They aren't	(they are not)	tak**ing** … .

Personalpronomen – Personal pronouns   Possessivbegleiter / Possessive determiners

Subjekt	Objekt	Possessive determiners
I	me	my
you	you	your
he	him	his
she	her	her
it	it	its
we	us	our
you	you	your
they	them	their

Der Satz – The sentence

	Subjekt	Hilfsverb	Verb	
	Nicola	is		Tessa's friend.
	She	can	speak	German and English.
	She		goes	to Islington Green.
	She	is	going	to visit Tessa now.

Fragewort	Hilfsverb	Subjekt	Verb	
	Can	you	see	Mr Clifton?
	Does	she	play	with the cat?
What	is	Tarkan	doing	in the kitchen?
Where	does	he	go	with his friend?
		Who	knows	her aunt?
Who	can	she	see?	

GRAMMAR

Fragen und verneinte Sätze mit *do / don't* und *does / doesn't*
Questions and negative sentences with *do / don't* and *does / doesn't*

Frage			Antwort	
Hilfsverb	Vollverb	Ergänzung	Hilfsverb + *not*	Vollverb
Do you	know	the band?	No, I **don't**	(know it).
Do your teachers	wear	school uniform?	No, they **don't**	(wear uniform).
Does Mrs Modi	like	computer games?	No, she **doesn't**	(like them).

Der *s*-Genitiv – The *s*-genitive

singular	Tessa**'s** mother	the girl**'s** books	Liz**'s** friends
plural	the Clifton**s'** house	the boy**s'** rooms	the children**'s** toys

Vergleiche mit *-er / -est* und *more / most*
Comparisons with *-er / -est* and *more / most*

Your house is **older than** our house. But it isn't the **oldest** house here. It isn't **as old as** Tony's house.

fast	fast**er**	(the) fast**est**	interesting	**more** interesting	(the) **most** interesting
nice	nic**er**	(the) nic**est**	difficult	**more** difficult	(the) **most** difficult
funny	funn**ier**	(the) funn**iest**	good	**better**	(the) **best**
			bad	**worse**	(the) **worst**

Die Zusammensetzungen von *some* und *any* – The compounds of *some* and *any*

Die Zusammensetzungen von *some* und *any* – *something, anybody, somewhere* usw. – werden nach den gleichen Regeln verwendet wie *some* und *any*.

bejahte Aussagen	Fragen	verneinte Aussagen
I want to buy **something** for Liam's birthday.	Can you think of **anything**?	No, sorry. I can't think of **anything**.
We must ask **somebody**.	Can you see **anybody**?	I'm sorry. I can't see **anybody**.
My T-shirt must be **somewhere**.	Is it **anywhere** in the kitchen?	No, it isn't. I can't find it **anywhere**.

must / mustn't / needn't

Must drückt aus, dass etwas notwendig ist oder sein muss. *Needn't* steht, wenn jemand etwas nicht zu tun braucht. *Mustn't* bedeutet, dass jemand etwas nicht tun sollte oder nicht tun darf.

Must I phone Dr Modi?	Milly **must** stay in the house.	The ships **must** stop dumping waste overboard.
No, you **needn't** phone him.	We **needn't** take her to the vet.	Holidaymakers **mustn't** drop rubbish on the beach.

GRAMMAR

Die vollendete Gegenwart – The present perfect

Das *present perfect* brauchst du, wenn du sagen willst, was jemand (nicht) gemacht hat. Dabei ist es nicht wichtig, wann etwas geschah, sondern dass das Ergebnis in der Gegenwart noch spürbar ist.
Bildung: *have / has + past participle (infinitive + -(e)d bei regelmäßigen Verben)*
have / has + past participle (bei unregelmäßigen Verben)

Have you **read** the book? – Yes, I **have read** this book. / No, I **haven't read** this book.

I **have**			**Have** I		No, I **haven't**	
You **have**			**Have** you		No, you **haven't**	
He **has**	clean**ed**		**Has** he	clean**ed**	No, he **hasn't**	clean**ed**
She **has**	mend**ed**	the car.	**Has** she	mend**ed** the car?	No, she **hasn't**	mend**ed** the car.
It **has**	seen		**Has** it	seen	No, it **hasn't**	seen
We **have**			**Have** we		No, we **haven't**	
You **have**			**Have** you		No, you **haven't**	
They **have**			**Have** they		No, they **haven't**	

⁺Die Vergangenheit (einfache Form) – The simple past

Das *simple past* verwendest du, wenn du sagen willst, was in der Vergangenheit (nicht) los war oder was jemand (nicht) getan hat. Die Handlung muss abgeschlossen sein. Bei Fragen und Verneinungen *did / didn't* nicht vergessen! Signalwörter: *yesterday, ago, last week / month / year, in 1998* usw.
Bildung: *infinitive + -(e)d bei regelmäßigen Verben*
simple past form bei unregelmäßigen Verben

Were you in Cornwall last year? – No, we **weren't**. We were in Scotland last year.
Where **did** you go last year? – We **went** to Scotland last year.

Aussage	Frage	Verneinung
I **was**	**Was** I	No, I **wasn't**
You **were**	**Were** you	No, you **weren't**
He **was**	**Was** he	No, he **wasn't**
She **was** in London last year.	**Was** she in London last year?	No, she **wasn't** in London.
It **was**	**Was** it	No, it **wasn't**
We **were**	**Were** we	No, we **weren't**
You **were**	**Were** you	No, you **weren't**
They **were**	**Were** they	No, they **weren't**

Aussage		Frage	Verneinung
Yesterday	I **saw** a film.	**Did** you see a film yesterday?	I **didn't** see a film yesterday.
	she visit**ed** her friends.	**Did** she visit her friends?	She **didn't** visit her friends.
	we play**ed** reggae music.	**Did** you play reggae music?	We **didn't** play reggae music.

Verbs

present		past	
usually / often	*just / now*	*just / already*	*all over now*
say / says	am / is / are saying	has / have said	said
make / makes	am / is / are making	has / have made	made
walk / walks	am / is / are walking	has / have walked	walked
write / writes	am / is / are writing	has / have written	wrote
help / helps	am / is / are helping	has / have helped	helped

GRAMMAR

Das *going to*-Futur – The going to-future

Das *going to-future* verwendest du, wenn du sagen willst, was jemand vorhat oder zu tun beabsichtigt. Es geht um kurzfristige Vorhaben für die nahe Zukunft.
Bildung: *am / is / are going to + infinitive*.

What are you **going to** do next? – I'm **going to** listen to my new CD.

I'm	**going to**	take	these things to the Assembly Hall.
What are you	**going to**	do	today?
David is	**going to**	take	some photos.
She is	**going to**	phone	her friend.
We're	**going to**	clean	our bikes.
They're	**going to**	play	tennis.

Verwechsle das *going to-future* nicht mit dem *present progressive*:
I'm **going to** go shopping. – Ich habe vor, einkaufen zu gehen. (= später)
I'm going shopping. – Ich gehe einkaufen. (= gerade jetzt)

⁺Das *will*-Futur – The will-future

Das *will-future* verwendest du, wenn du sagen willst, was geschehen wird, aber nicht mehr beeinflusst werden kann (z.B. Wettervorhersage). Außerdem steht das *will-future*, wenn eine feste Verabredung vorliegt oder du spontan zu etwas bereit bist, ohne es geplant zu haben.

Will the weather be fine? – Yes, it **will** be nice.

			Will	it, you, they, …?		
I					I	
You		When		he …?	You	
He		What		she …?	He	
She					She	
It	**'ll (will)** ….	How	**will**	it …?	It	**won't (will not)** ….
We		Where		you …?	We	
You		Why		they …?	You	
They					They	

Future

	going to	will
say	going to say	will say
make	going to make	will make
walk	going to walk	will walk
write	going to write	will write
help	going to help	will help

⁺Das Gerundium – The gerund

Reading is fun. – Liz enjoys **reading** comics.

subject			object
Reading	is fun.		
Juggling	is my hobby.		
Climbing	can be dangerous.		
Playing	on the beach is great.		

I	like		**reading.**
Do you	enjoy		**reading** too?
We	love		**walking.**
Liz doesn't	like		**running.**
Mrs Clifton	hates		**swimming.**

Das *gerund* kann Subjekt oder Objekt eines Satzes sein. Als Objekt steht es oft nach Verben der Vorliebe (*like, love, enjoy*) oder der Abneigung (*hate*).
Bildung: *verb + -ing*
Die *-ing* Form kann entweder ein *gerund* oder die *progressive form* des Verbs sein.

gerund after adjectives and prepositions

Are you good at **running**?
She is proud of **writing** some stories.
Liam is crazy about **sending** e-mails.

Check-out – Lösungen

Unit 1

1. 2. ticket / three tickets 3. taxi / four taxis 4. instrument / five instruments 5. guitar / six guitars 6. window / seven windows 7. friend / eight friends 8. picture / nine pictures
2. 1. I, I 2. She 3. we 4. you 5. He 6. She
3. 1. Tessa and Tony 2. keyboard are her 3. is a Turkish 4. a singer too. 5. are the two 6. is the reporter
4. airport, baggage, car, departure, example, fun, game, hotel, instrument, keyboarder, letter, magazine, name, open, picture, reporter, singer, taxi, welcome, yes

Unit 2

1. 1. Yes, you can. / Of course! 2. Oh, sorry! / Oh! 3. That's nice. / That's funny. 4. Sure. / No problem. 5. No, there isn't. / Yes, there is. 6. Why not? / That's OK. 7. Thank you. / Thanks. 8. What? / Why not? 9. Good idea! / OK! 10. No, it isn't. / Yes, it is.
2. 1. The Cliftons have got a new car. 2. Sandra has got a guitar. 3. Liz has got a dog. 4. Mrs Braden has got a new computer. 5. Mrs Clifton and Mr Braden have got an antique shop. 6. Jimmy has got some new CDs.
3. Across: 2. garage 4. fireplace 7. piano 8. stairs 9. window 11. tree 12. attic 14. lot 15. trees 16. hall 17. houses 19. no 20. living room 22. flat 24. know 25. rooms 26. now 27. new
   Down: 1. table 2. garden 3. beds 4. flowers 5. pictures 6. kitchen 10. bathrooms 13. chairs 18. sofa 20. lawn 21. roof 23. low

Unit 3

1. basketball, cafeteria, Design (and Technology), English, French, Geography, History, IT (Information Technology), job, kid, lesson, Maths, number, open, PE (Physical Education), quiz, role play, Science, teacher, unit, volleyball, week, –, year, –
2. 1. seventy 2. colour 3. homework 4. owners 5. over there 6. lunch // The word is: school.
4. 1. Do you like cats? 2. Do you play football? 3. Do you go to school? 4. Do you read lots of comics? 5. Do you go to bed early? 6. Do you listen to music? 7. Do you often watch TV? 8. Do you have assembly at school? 9. Do you like hot dogs? 10. Do you live in a house or a flat?

Unit 4

1. 1. stop at a red traffic light 2. dial a number on a mobile phone 3. open the door with a key 4. see the time on the clock 5. walk on a bed of nails 6. find the way on a map 7. sit at the top of a double decker bus
2. 1. … is feeding the birds. 2. … is selling newspapers. 3. … are sitting around and feeding the birds. 4. … are watching a musical. 5. … are playing the drums. 6. … are just lying on the grass / are having a picnic / are looking at magazines. 7. … are buying things.
3. 2. … – No, they aren't. 3. Are Liz and Liam clapping? – Yes, they are. 4. Is Tarkan writing a postcard? – No, he isn't. 5. Is Mr Clifton reading? – Yes, he is. 6. Is the bird singing? – No, it isn't.

Unit 5

1. *Lösungsvorschläge* 1. They are £20 each. 2. Yes, of course. Here you are. 3. I would like a green one, please. 4. Sure. Have a look in that box over there. 5. You can have two for £8. 6. Try the bookshop. 7. You can go by Underground. 8. I bought some sweets. 9. It was too expensive there. 10. I took the Underground. 11. Vanilla, please. 12. I don't like chocolate. Two bananas, please.
2. 1. videos 2. shoes 3. computers 4. scarves 5. chairs 6. clothes 7. instruments 8. jewelry *(AE)* 9. calendars 10. watches 11. glasses 12. leather 13. food 14. sports 15. sweets // department store
3. 1. Big Ben, Empire State Building 2. Harrods, Macy's 3. HMV, Tiffany's 4. Islington, SoHo 5. Islington High Street, Orchard Street 6. Camden Lock market, Orchard Street market 7. chips, pastrami sandwiches 8. café, deli 9. pounds, dollars 10. tube, subway 11. rock music, jazz 12. CDs, jeans
4. 1. Harrods sell(s) everything but it's very expensive there. 2. Macy's is one of the biggest department stores in the USA. 3. At Tiffany's you can get all kinds of jewelry. 4. HMV is a computer shop. You can buy all kinds of computer games there. 5. It's a pet shop. It sells pets and food for pets.